PRAISE FOR *HOW WINNERS SELL*

"**I**f you want to master the art of selling, don't read this book. USE this book!"

Anthony Parinello
Author, *Selling to VITO* and *Think and Sell like a CEO*

"**H**ow *Winners Sell* is clear, it's concise, it's reality-based. Smart salespeople will adopt the 21 strategies contained in this book and dramatically increase their income. Not having this book may cost you a hundred times its price in the first year."

Gerhard Gschwandtner
Founder and Publisher
***Selling Power* magazine**

"**D**ave's ideas introduce fresh strategies and tactics for our dynamic times. A highly recommended read for our members and their teams."

Willis Turner, CSE
COO
Sales & Marketing Executives-International, Inc.

"**S**traight to the point, easy to read. Each chapter adds specific value to any selling opportunity. The great salespeople will use these strategies."

Christopher Larsen
EVP, Global Field Operations & Marketing, Verticalnet
Former President, SAP America, Inc.

"**T**his book is a real treasure trove of proven, practical ideas you can use to increase your sales immediately — in any market."

Brian Tracy
Author, *Advanced Selling Strategies*

"**A** winner! Dave Stein tells us what to do and how to do it — step-by-step — from selling to top-level executives to leveraging the Internet as a selling tool. A must for selling products or services in today's hypercompetitive marketplace. Required reading for my team."

> **John Zobel**
> **Director, Global National Accounts**
> **Qwest Communications**

"**T**he ideal 21st-century guide to selling. The focus on studying and understanding your customers, their competition, and their industry is invaluable in closing sales."

> **Rocco Campanelli**
> **Executive VP**
> **RCM Technologies, Inc.**

"**M**any business books are too theoretical. This one was easy to read and worth my time. I don't say that about many business books."

> **Tony Friscia**
> **President and CEO**
> **AMR Research, Inc.**

"**T**his book provides you with a much-needed road map for today's business world. Using these strategies will greatly increase the success possibilities in your own venture or professional career."

> **Luis Fernando Pardo**
> **President, Delta–Latin America Market Advisors**
> **Former President, Eberhard Faber de Venezuela**
> **Former Vice President Latin America for Sanford**
> **Corporation (a Newell Rubbermaid Corporation)**

"**H**ow *Winners Sell* is money in the bank. These are not just 'proven' strategies — they are SALES WINNING strategies."

Jeffrey Gitomer
Author of *The Sales Bible* and *Customer Satisfaction is Worthless, Customer Loyalty is Priceless*

"**D**ave's book saves busy executives the effort of wading through lengthy management tomes to pick up the tips and strategies they need. It's full of quick, helpful advice that managers can put to use immediately. What a refreshing difference!"

Melinda Ligos
Editor in Chief
***Sales & Marketing Management* magazine**

"**T**ake this book seriously! You will achieve maximum sales results and feel good about the value you bring to your clients. The tactics can be put into action immediately. Great resource for sales reps and their managers."

Paulette DesCoteaux
Sales Vice President
Pitney Bowes Supply Chain Solutions

"**I**'ve read many 'how to' books. This one is definitely at the top of my list."

Diane Mitchell
Senior Marketing Manager
Bayer Corporation

"**C**olorful metaphors and examples demonstrate today's immutable laws of selling. Shows you the money! Helps you access the top and get inside."

Robert Kraut
Brand Manager
General Motors

"Chock-full of pearls of wisdom. Every successful accountant, lawyer, consultant — anyone in business — can benefit from the ideas and information in the 21 strategies."

Wayne Cooper
CEO
Kennedy Information, Inc.

"I have worked with Dave in a variety of capacities for fifteen years and am delighted to see him sharing his proven sales methodologies through the publishing of *How Winners Sell*."

Gerry O'Connell
CEO
Entuity, Inc.

"A 'hands-on' trainer to lead the reader through the steps necessary for future success."

Bruce Kopkin
President
Lorentzen & Wettre

"Dave has put together all the elements of a great sales process. He brings to the table the tools for a successful sales campaign and ways to utilize them with proficiency."

Mike Clayville
VP Business Development
ecFood

"Provides insight and information on how salespeople can achieve the transition to businesspeople. The writing style is clear, relevant, and to the point."

Barbara Geraghty
Sales Trainer
Author of *Visionary Selling*

"Too many books on selling have been written by 'armchair quarterbacks' with little field experience. Dave is truly a master of the art of strategic sales. He has produced a practical guide that will be must reading for my team."

Gary Davies
General Manager
Ariba Canada, Inc.

"You instantly know that Dave Stein has 'been there and done that.' You get the sense that Dave is there with you providing one-on-one coaching on your own sales challenges. Why make mistakes that cost you the deal? Learn from the author, who has seen and studied what it takes to win."

LaVon Koerner
CEO
Revenue Storm

"Provides clear, actionable guidance that can impact sales immediately. An excellent job delivering practical, high-impact advice."

Christopher E. Fountain
President & CEO
Digital Paper Corporation

"How Winners Sell will improve the effectiveness of any sales organization. A roadmap for success, well thought out and easy to understand. Should be the fundamental model for sales managers wanting to improve overall sales performance."

Rick Dunlop
President
BTG Americas Inc.

How Winners Sell

21 Proven Strategies to Outsell Your Competition and Win the Big Sale

Dave Stein

BARD PRESS
Austin ▶ Atlanta

How Winners Sell

21 Proven Strategies to Outsell Your Competition and Win the Big Sale

Bard Press
An Imprint of Longstreet Press
2974 Hardman Court
Atlanta, GA 30305
404-254-0110, fax 404-254-0116
www.bardpress.com

Ordering Information
To order additional copies, contact your local bookstore or call 800-945-3132.

ISBN 1-885167-55-5 hardcover

Library of Congress Cataloging-in-Publication Data
Stein, Dave, 1947-
     How winners sell : 21 proven strategies to outsell your competition and win the big sale / Dave Stein.
                    p.   cm.
     Includes index.
     ISBN 1-885167-55-5 (hardcover)
     1. Selling. I. Title.

     HF5438.25 .S734 2002
     658.8'5--dc21   2001052700

Author Dave Stein may be contacted as follows:
    phone: 845-621-4100
    e-mail: info@TheSteinAdvantage.com
    websites: www.TheSteinAdvantage.com, www.HowWinnersSell.com

Credits
Editor: Jeff Morris
Proofreaders: Deborah Costenbader, Bobbie Jo Sims, Luke Torn
Index: Linda Webster
Cover design: Hespenheide Design
Cartoon art: Cartoon Resource
Author photo: Peter Tenzer Studio (www.portfolios.com/petertenzer)
Text design/production: Jeff Morris

First printing: March 2002

For Vivian, Jessica, and Robyn

▶ Contents

**PART 3.
GETTING INTO
THE GAME**

**PART 4.
THE STUFF
WINNERS DO**

**PART 5.
THE DECISION
AND BEYOND**

11

△

What Worked Then Doesn't Work Now

Times have changed.

You're a professional salesperson, selling business-to-business. You've been in this profession for a while. Long enough to know that it's changed — a lot. Long enough to know that making a living in sales is both more exciting and more uncertain than ever before.

Your industry, whatever it might be, is more competitive than ever. New products and services come out faster and change more frequently. People seem to know more about price, quality, capability, reliability, and alternatives.

Your customers are more demanding: they want more information, more options, bigger discounts, better service. They want to talk to you when *they* want to talk to you.

Remember all those sales principles and strategies you learned in school? All those approaches and techniques you read in books? All those tips, tricks, and secrets you picked up when you were new on the job and learning fast? Gone.

Well, not exactly gone, but changed. Different. Some of them still work, but you have to think about them differently, use them in new ways. Others, you've already figured out, are now as stale as week-old bread.

Yesterday's answers just don't seem to fit today's selling environment. They don't answer today's questions:

▶ How do you differentiate yourself?

▶ How do you keep people from treating what you sell as a commodity — so you can compete on something other than price?

▶ How do you build credibility?

▶ How do you survive as a sales professional? How do you thrive?

Buyers are smarter these days. They know a lot about you and your company, and they know how to find out more: your fees, your prices, weaknesses in your offering, your financial condition, your unhappy customers. They know all the approaches salespeople have used on them over the years, and they know how to take advantage. They're aware that a lot of the sales talk they hear is just hype. And what they know makes it harder and harder for you to compete. It's a buyer's market.

Did I say hype? You bet. It's more competitive out there than it's ever been — more companies hyping more and more stuff to the same people. Look at today's business-to-consumer marketing: automakers' deep discounts, airlines' fare wars, telecoms' come-ons, broadcasters' program teasers. It's the same in business-to-business sales. There are more companies than ever before, often trying to sell very similar products to the same businesses, and your clients know it. It's hypercompetitive, and it's a new ballgame.

What's happening? Why has competition become so frantic, so cutthroat? Well, for those of you who have just awakened from a long nap or returned home from visiting another planet, I've got news: there's been a revolution. Thanks to a tiny, inexpensive flake known as the microchip, access to information has been totally transformed.

"The least you could have done was to put
a new ribbon in your typewriter."

Remember the square pink "While You Were Out" note? If you do, it doesn't mean you're an old-timer. We've gone at warp speed from pencil and paper and snail mail, to telephone answering machines and faxes, through voice mail and cell phones, all the way to e-mail — and now we have online PDAs (personal digital assistants) that give us access to all messages, all the time. Each step in this revolution has brought us closer to being perpetually in touch: $60 \times 60 \times 24 \times 7 \times 52$.

Companies you sell for, as well as companies you sell to, know you are reachable anytime, anywhere — at work, on the road, at home, in the shower, at the Little League game, even on vacation. So everyone expects you to be on call, available, and informed — your employers, your clients, your prospects, as well as your family and friends. (A good friend of mine, who is a superb sales executive, tells his sales professionals, with a glint of humor in his eyes: "You can take a vacation anytime you want, so long as it isn't during the last three months of any quarter.")

Swift and sure person-to-person communication is one prong of the revolution that's transforming our profession. The other — the really big one — is the Internet.

Ready access to information is a powerful tool. People who might buy from you can now go online and, in a matter of minutes, find out everything they need to know about your company, your products or services, your customer satisfaction track record, your competitors and their products and customers, and what companies in their own and other industries are doing to solve the same problems and meet the same needs. The Internet gives your prospects innumerable sources of free or cheap information about products, services, markets, technology, and people.

This information revolution has you, the sales professional, caught in a box. You are expected to provide whatever information the client needs, and more —not tomorrow, but

"The Internet is still in its infancy. Over the next five years, we'll see enormous technological leaps that will make the Net more and more pervasive in our work and in our lives."

— STATEMENT AGREED TO BY 93 PERCENT OF RESPONDENTS TO A SURVEY BY *FAST COMPANY* MAGAZINE (MARCH 2001)

right now! If you are unable to provide it, your client can easily find someone who will do the job. And so can your boss.

You've heard that time is money. Well, information is big money. Even if you're not selling technology or technical support services, in the era of the Internet you have to view information as a liquid asset. If you don't know the value of information, where to get it, and how to use it to win sales, you'll find it tough to stay in business. Here's why:

▶ Your clients have the goods on your company. You can't tell them much they don't already know. You may be out of the running before you walk in the door, before you can even respond to their request for proposal (RFP).

▶ Your clients have the lowdown on their own customers, suppliers, and competitors. This gives them an advantage over you, unless you know as much (or more) and can present a credible business case.

▶ Your clients can easily obtain information about products or services that compete with yours. This has the effect of turning what you're selling into a mere commodity, competing in terms of price alone.

Bad news for us sales professionals, you say. Yes, it is. But I've given you the bad news first to get it out of the way.

Now, the good news: Once you understand the power of the information revolution, you can exploit it to its fullest. It's like any resource: if you can make the best use of it and become more adept at bringing its benefits to your customers, you'll come out ahead of your competition.

One point in your favor: there's so much information available now that the job of finding, evaluating, managing, and using it has become a limiting factor. Your clients don't have time to filter, analyze, and integrate what's relevant from all the data that's bombarding them. It's like trying to drink water from a fire hose.

This "infoglut" is a golden opportunity for you. It gives you an opening to become a thought leader or trusted advisor for your client. You take on the job of sorting, interpreting, and winnowing the facts; you condense and present what's relevant to the company's bottom line. In the process you become a valued coach, teacher, researcher, explorer, guide, and catalyst for change. Executives grow to depend on your experience, your commitment, and your ability to contribute to their company's success.

For an outsider, winning the position of trusted advisor is not easy — believe me, I know. But it *can* be done. To be a winner, you have to differentiate yourself from your competition in the way you use generally available information for the benefit of your client. You have to demonstrate that you provide real value to your client, and especially to key people in the company. And you have to be better at it than anyone else.

This is not a totally new idea, of course. Savvy sales professionals have "consulted" with their clients for decades. But how, when, and to whom should you provide the value of your expertise? This requires new thinking. To become a sales winner in the information age, you have to learn

▶ how to manage information as working capital

▶ how to protect your sales proposition against competitors' inroads

▶ how to establish credibility with your prospect

▶ how to gain and maintain access to key people

▶ how to position yourself as uniquely valuable to your prospect

The speed with which the business world has embraced the information revolution has caught a lot of salespeople off guard. Unless you sell for one of the leading-edge technology providers, you probably don't fully comprehend how it has changed and is changing your profession. I am going to remedy that — with this book.

If you are already successful at implementing this vision of sales success, *How Winners Sell* will affirm your strengths and enable you to focus on areas you can leverage for even greater sales success.

17
△

How This Book Will Help You

My purpose in writing *How Winners Sell* is to present a comprehensive plan with specific strategies and tactics that will give you an effective and lasting sales advantage. Here's what I will provide and how it will help you be a sales winner:

▶ I will explain what new skills you need in order to thrive in today's hypercompetitive business-to-business marketplace.

▶ I will propose new ways to apply skills that you've already learned to give yourself more credibility with today's tougher, more informed, more experienced buyer.

▶ I will provide new insights into deciding which sales opportunities are worth pursuing so you can focus your attention, energy, and resources on deals you can win.

▶ I will coach you on leading a virtual sales team, so you can overcome organizational inhibitors that may be keeping them from achieving their potential.

▶ I will give you a template for creating simple yet powerful sales plans that will dramatically improve your win rate, job security, and earning power.

▶ I will show you what is important to top executives so that you can gain and maintain access at that level when you need to — or at other levels, when appropriate.

▶ I will describe how to understand and discuss your customers' stated and unstated business issues in order to increase their interest and participation.

▶ I will suggest ways to earn privileges not available to competitors that will bring you insights into how to win sales.

▶ I will show how to recruit influential people within your accounts and train them to sell on your behalf when you are not there.

▶   I will demonstrate how to control the time, the place, and the rules under which you will compete, so you can outsell even the largest competitor.

▶   I will tell you how to learn crucial information about your competition that will help you win.

▶   I will explain how to increase the size of your opportunities, get prospects to close sooner, and spend fewer resources winning them, thus producing bigger commission checks for you, more accurate forecasting for your manager, and higher margins for your company.

▶   I will tell how to establish mutually profitable, personally rewarding relationships with your clients and colleagues.

PLANNING IS CRUCIAL

When it comes to winning sales, I believe in a logical and straightforward process that starts with the general and ends with the specific:

▶   First, gain a thorough understanding of the prospect's business environment — the conditions and circumstances that determine what the prospect will ultimately buy.

▶   Next, identify your intention. In selling, we usually talk in terms of an objective rather than a goal.

▶   Once your intent is clear and unequivocal, design the strategy by which you expect to achieve your objective.

▶   Finally, devise a set of tactics — the tasks, events, and steps required to successfully execute your strategy.

Notice that I'm following this structure in the book itself, with a slight modification: I have set a goal in this case, not an objective. First, I described your selling environment, as I believe it exists today. Next, I stated the goal for this book. In sales planning, we use objectives, which are generally expressed as hard numbers. Goals are loftier, but softer and less specific.

The core of *How Winners Sell* consists of twenty-one chapters, each containing one proven strategy for achieving your goal: outselling your competition and winning the big sale. Why have I chosen this structure? Because I know you are busy and will probably have time to read only one chapter at a time. You'll see that I have presented the strategies in the order in which you will use them when preparing and executing a sales campaign. Within each chapter, I present tactics that will help you execute the strategy.

If your approach to selling has always been unplanned, you may feel daunted by the prospect of devising and executing a strategy by using specific tactics. Think of it this way: as a sales professional, you're not just the foot soldier, you're the general, too. Without both, few battles are won.

What It's All About

> **STRATEGY #1. UNDERSTAND THE TIMELESS TRUTH ABOUT SALES: IT'S ALL ABOUT MONEY**

Why are you in business?

When I ask my clients this question, I get different answers. Some say their companies provide places where people can work, improve their standard of living, and build rewarding careers. Others talk about how their products and services make life better for their customers. Still others remind me of their company's place in the great economic

machine; it helps make the nation strong, they say, and besides, look how much we contribute to charities and to our
communities.

All this is true, of course, and admirable. But when they
talk of these benefits as their companies' main reason for
being, my clients are fooling themselves. The main reason
for doing business boils down to this:

It's all about money.

Sure, a company should reward its employees, contribute to the community, and make the nation stronger. But if
a company does not eventually generate a consistent profit,
it will not stay around long enough to make anyone's life
better — except, perhaps, the bankruptcy attorneys'.

To top-level executives, achieving their business plan
ultimately comes down to money. They may measure it as
economic value added, return on equity, return on assets, return on investment, top-line
revenue, margin, contribution, increased market share, earnings per share, a reputation for
quality, quickness to market, or something else,
but it will always relate to money, counted one
way or another.

The same principle lies behind achieving
great business-to-business sales. If, as a sales
professional, you can show your clients exactly how, and by how much, you will increase
their revenues, decrease their expenses, or
both, you will establish a solid basis for doing
business with them.

Some sales professionals like to point out
cases where you cannot cost-justify your solution. Suppose
that what you provide is a product or service that enables
companies to comply with a government regulation. If doing business with you will keep your client from paying a
fine, closing facilities, or losing customers, you have a plat-
form upon which you can build a strong business case.

> If, as a sales profes-
> sional, you can
> show your clients
> exactly how, and
> by how much, you
> will increase their
> revenues, decrease
> their expenses, or
> both, you will
> establish a solid
> basis for doing
> business with them.

The winningest salespeople are those who keep the bottom line foremost in their minds. They will tell you that in order to be consistently successful, you must build upon the single most important timeless truth of sales:

It's all about money.

MONEY FOR WHAT?

CFOs recognize two basic types of expenditures: necessary and value-added. Value-added expenditures, or investments, bring a financial return by increasing revenues or decreasing expenses. Necessary expenses, on the other hand, are costs such as payroll services, regulatory compliance, insurance, and real estate. The goal of the CFO when evaluating and procuring services or products from a supplier on the "necessary" side is to minimize the drain on the company's resources. That's where vendors of outsourcing services can win. Offer a reliable, cost-effective, turnkey service, and you're halfway to a sale.

A CEO with whom I do business runs a public high-tech company. He believes his primary job is to increase shareholder value by improving earnings per share (EPS). He sees every product enhancement, big win, marketing campaign, securities analyst comment, or loss of a proven salesperson in terms of its impact on the company's earnings per share. His people receive bonuses when the company achieves its quarterly EPS goals. So when I get a chance to present a proposal to meet his business needs, such as new selling strategies against a tough competitor, you can see how I'll approach him: right to his EPS. That's how he counts his company's money, and that's how I position what I sell him.

Another client counts its money differently. As a wholly owned subsidiary of a public corporation, this company's success is directly proportional to the profit it contributes to the parent corporation. The subsidiary is generating cash, but the parent company is not doing as well as expected. I know exactly how to position my proposals to these folks. It's not earnings per share they seek, nor revenue growth. They need to generate cash, and cash is the measurement I use when I position the contribution I can make.

In an article published in *Fast Company* (March 2001), well-known business strategist Michael Porter says:

> Sound strategy starts with having the right goal. And I argue that the only goal that can support a sound strategy is superior profitability. If you don't start with that goal and seek it pretty directly, you will quickly be led to actions that will undermine strategy. If your goal is anything but profitability — if it's to be big, or to grow fast, or to become a technology leader — you'll hit problems.

Appendix 1, "How to Get Your Project Funded," will give you a detailed explanation of why and how investment decisions are made for products and services that you may be selling.

If what you're selling is not perceived as strategic or mission critical by your market, it's your job (with help from your company's marketing team) to find out what specific contribution your product or service can make to your customer or client's business plan.

If you've been in enterprise or corporate sales for a time, you'll know that so far as your ability to gather information about your prospect's financial position is concerned, there

---

TACTIC: Make a business-oriented portal your home page. Set aside twenty minutes each morning to scan the news about your top three customers, clients, or prospects and their top three customers, suppliers, and competitors, including current stock quotes and financial information. Also scan the news about the industry into which you are selling and more general business news — domestic first, then international. Look to our website, www.HowWinnersSell.com, for the latest in web-based and other resources to support your selling efforts.

---

are two types of companies: publicly held and privately held. These categories differ greatly in the amount of information available.

PUBLICLY HELD CORPORATIONS

In the hands of a knowledgeable, disciplined sales professional, the Internet is the most effective tool for learning
about a publicly held corporation's financial position and
business plan (discipline is required to avoid surfing the
day away). In the United States, we can thank the Securities
and Exchange Commission (SEC) for requiring more and
better financial information than ever from public companies. All the standard financial reports about most public
companies are available free of charge on the Internet at
www.freeedgar.com.

As you read through the financial reports, such as the
10-Q (issued quarterly, containing financial results and significant changes or events) and the 10-K (an annual report
that includes the outlook for the future), you can begin to
discern aspects of how targeted companies see themselves,

TACTIC: Read the 10-Qs and 10-Ks of your most important customers and
their most troublesome competitors. Focus on financial measurements and
business strategy, then base your discussions with executives and senior
managers on these.

---

their marketplace, their industry, their challenges, risks, and
competition, and their financial position going forward.

PRIVATELY HELD CORPORATIONS

It's harder to get information about privately held companies from outside sources. The owners and managers tend
to take the word "private" very seriously. The only thing
readily available may be a company or product brochure,
but you can often search for the company name on the Internet and follow the links for nuggets of valuable information. There are many fee-based websites, such as

www.hoovers.com, that have information on privately held companies. In general, though, don't expect to find the kind of information about your private client's or prospect's financial position or business condition that the SEC requires public companies to report.

In my experience, the best information about a private company — how it makes and counts its money, who "wins" when there's more of it, and how you can contribute to its profitability — come from two sources:

▶ sales professionals who work for other suppliers (who don't compete with you), and

▶ people in the company you can persuade to talk.

As you know, salespeople have a unique perspective on what's happening out there in their marketplace. They know their company's strengths, weaknesses, wins, losses, and in many cases what needs to be done, at least in the short to

What you need to know about your prospect and how to find it out are covered in chapter 11.

TACTIC: One effective way to start getting information about a prospective client company is by calling the head office and getting the name and number of the salesperson for the territory where you work, then calling that person. Keep the conversation simple: "Jim? My name is Dave Stein. I'm a sales rep for The Stein Advantage, and I'm researching your company for a presentation I'll be doing for Mr. Reeve and Ms. Maxwell on February third. I'd love to get your perspective on opportunities and challenges in your marketplace. I won't ask for any information you'd be uncomfortable discussing. Would you be willing to meet me for a beer after work later this week? Perhaps I can give you some sales leads or other information that might advance your selling efforts."

medium term, to bring in more revenue. That said, whatever information you get by interviewing a sales rep is by no means the final word on any aspect of your prospect's business. Like information from any other single source, it needs to be corroborated by others in the account.

This method of getting information works more often than not. Many sales winners have told me that they got not only the information they were looking for but a few leads as well. In one or two cases, they formed long-term relationships.

Outside of sales, how do you get others in a company to give you the financial and other information you need to position your product or service to the decision makers? Answer: by building trust. Trust is a product of integrity and competence. If you exhibit integrity, your prospects know you will always do what is in their best interests and you're willing to be held accountable. Being competent means you can answer their questions correctly — even questions they haven't thought of yet. When you build trust, you earn the

---

TACTIC: Devise your own methods of gaining information about privately held corporations you sell to. These methods will depend on the industry, the size and culture of the companies, and your own network of business contacts within installed accounts.

---

right to ask what you need to know so that down the road you can give them a proposal that will provide maximum value for their business.

STRENGTH IN KNOWLEDGE

Let's not lose sight of the point here. It's important to know the financial position of any company you intend to sell to: Are they making or losing money? Do they pay their bills on time? Will they pay cash or lease your products? But the real message to you is this: You need to know how — and by how much — your product or service can contribute to that company's ability to make more money or spend less money or to mitigate potentially costly risk. And in order to know that, you need to have a clear picture of the company's financial position today, what it was last quarter and last year, and what the company and the analysts who cover it expect its financial position to be in the future.

△

When you completely understand your prospect's past, current, and projected financial picture and can use this knowledge to persuade an executive that an investment of $1.00 in your product or service will bring his company $4.37 in additional profits within twelve months, you are

well beyond simply getting his attention. But these numbers must be real, and your prospect must be shown they are achievable with minimal risk.

Remember: It's all about money. All the relationship building, competitive positioning, and great negotiating skills in the world will not get you very far if you have not given your prospect solid, measurable business reasons to work

"The buck stops with the guy who signs the checks."

— RUPERT MURDOCH

with you. If you understand this and live by it, you've mastered Strategy #1; you've laid the foundation for your sales success and for mastering the other twenty strategies. You may not see this strategy as critical, since it is not a sales skill per se, but it will help you maintain the right mindset

> **TACTIC:** If you don't think you can position your product and service financially at the highest levels of the department, division, or enterprise into which you are selling, take a look at your current clients. Talk to a few of the people who signed on with your product or service — the people whose money it was or whose project or initiative it was. They will tell you in very clear terms why they made the investment. They may call it something else, but their purpose was to increase revenues, decrease expenses, mitigate risk, or all three.

when you are implementing the other strategies. Strategy #1 is a business skill, and, almost ironically, it is being a businessperson, not a salesperson, that will propel you to new levels of effectiveness and financial reward in your selling career.

Read more on this topic in chapter 5.

Part

1

Retooling Yourself to Win

Let's probe into the inventory of skills, attitudes, and behaviors of the consistently effective and successful sales winners. These are the people who have been able to perform regardless of what might be distracting their colleagues and competitors. Like sailboat skippers catching the wind in their sails, they have managed to leverage forces that are out of their control and use them to their own ends.

These advantaged performers seem to navigate their way to success with most of the sales opportunities they pursue. They are CEOs of their own virtual sales corporations, evaluating, planning, executing, directing, probing, positioning, building relationships, competing, negotiating, learning, advising, and taking responsibility for everything that happens in their sales campaigns.

Lisa Napolitano, president and CEO of the Strategic Account Management Association (SAMA), listed for me the jobs for which she believes today's strategic account manager is responsible:

- ▶ Administrator
- ▶ Communicator
- ▶ Consultant
- ▶ Diplomat
- ▶ Leader
- ▶ Missionary
- ▶ Motivator
- ▶ Negotiator
- ▶ Ombudsman
- ▶ Organizer
- ▶ Problem Solver
- ▶ Professional
- ▶ Relationship Builder
- ▶ Strategist
- ▶ Trainer
- ▶ Visionary

Sounds like the job description for a CEO, doesn't it? How well you perform these and other roles will determine how consistently you achieve sales success. To retool yourself for winning, you have to get an unbiased assessment of your skills, attitudes, and behaviors, then create and execute a series of simple strategic plans to achieve your goals in each area.

For example, if you believe that being able to read and interpret financial statements is a critical skill for gaining the advantage in selling, and it's a skill you don't have, here's how you would develop it:

Situation assessment: Interpreting financial statements is a key skill, and one that I don't have.

Objective: Learn how to read and interpret key financial reports by March 15.

Strategy: Attend a class on the subject.

Tactics:
1. Get recommendations for alternative classes.
2. Schedule time in my calendar.
3. Allocate funds for course fee.
4. Arrange transportation to and from the class.

Part 1 of *How Winners Sell* is about what's inside — that is, what inner resources you have available to draw on, and how you can develop the ones you need. When you have completed this part of the book

▶ you will see the importance of objectivity and the risks associated with wishful thinking.

▶ you will have had an opportunity to evaluate your relationship with change.

▶ you will know the critical skills that winners consistently demonstrate.

▶ you will have learned about effective communication in the information age.

▶ you will understand the importance of business and industry knowledge in competitive selling.

▶ you will begin to see things with a competitive state of mind.

As you read through part 1 of *How Winners Sell,* commit to improving the skills, attitudes, and behaviors you need to outsell the competition and win the big sale.

"Oh, that's just Mr. Tompkins doing his
'looking at myself with a clear objective eye.'"

Chapter 2

Can You Handle the Truth?

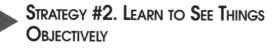

STRATEGY #2. LEARN TO SEE THINGS OBJECTIVELY

One of the most important skills winners have in common is the ability to see things objectively. Objectivity is critical for sales success. It gives us the ability to determine the truth and to handle any situation appropriately. Winning sales requires both outward-focused objectivity — a realistic picture of our true position in a sales campaign — and inward-focused objectivity, a clear-eyed assessment of our own skills and capabilities.

Keep in mind, however, that in the real world, objectivity is relative, not absolute. No person, however wide-awake and self-aware, can ever be totally objective about everything and everyone — especially himself. J. M. Barrie said, "We don't see things as they are, we see things as *we* are."

Experience is the best teacher of objectivity. Novice salespeople are often optimists; they have to be, to face all that rejection and keep coming back for more. They look for any nuance, any signal upon which they can build the belief that somewhere, somehow, there is business for them to win. Not only can't they assess a situation objectively, they generally don't see their own weaknesses. They are unconscious incompetents, unaware of their own deficiencies.

Even as they mature and gain experience, some salespeople continue to be wishful thinkers with "happy ears." They cannot — or will not — face the facts as they are; instead, they put a positive spin on anything they tell their bosses, their customers, and ultimately (or perhaps primarily) themselves. In other instances, salespeople deliberately avoid learning the truth. Like ostriches with their heads in the sand, they feel that if they don't ask the question, they can't get the bad news. These are defense mechanisms salespeople use, often unconsciously, out of fear of some real or perceived threat. (Sometimes salespeople don't know the difference between bad news and good news, but that's another issue.)

Inward-Focused Objectivity

Winners have the ability to accurately assess their own strengths and weaknesses, and the will to acknowledge them.

"Denial ain't just a river in Egypt."
— Mark Twain

To winners, everything is open to examination: the skills they have or have not developed over their years of selling, the personal traits they were born with, the behaviors they exhibit every day.

These sales professionals are constantly reassessing themselves — determining where they stand, where they need to be to sustain their success, and how they are going to get there. They work constantly on areas needing improvement and, in the meantime, seek help from others to compensate for weaknesses in these skills, traits, and behaviors. They understand that, especially in our world of constant change, what may have contributed to their success then doesn't necessarily get the job done now.

Winners know that their own weaknesses can jeopardize the success of an entire sales campaign. A tendency to panic when things aren't going well, for instance, or to be a lone wolf, unable or unwilling to work other members of a team, can be fatal when pursing a complex, competitive sales opportunity.

> Winners seek the truth. They understand that it is a vital element of their success.

Outward-Focused Objectivity

Winners seek the truth. They understand that it is a vital element of their success. Top sales professionals are consistently objective about the world around them, especially the true state of their sales campaigns and the motivations, intentions, and capabilities of the people they're selling to.

When I am called in to help a company win a difficult sales campaign, my number-one task is to find out how objective the sales rep is about the sales opportunity. It's not my practice to meet the prospect, so until I can speak with other team members, I have to base my assessment solely on what the rep tells me. If that rep is not objective, I can't help him.

Suppose I ask the rep the color of the prospect's building and he tells me it's gray. Can I assume it's gray? Maybe it's green and he's colorblind. I can't know for sure unless I have some other source of information. If another sales rep tells me she's got the inside track with a prospect, I can't know whether that's true, from her observations alone, unless I've determined that she can be objective.

Deception is a common practice. Whether to spare your feelings or to get a better negotiating position with another supplier, the prospect may string you along, making you think the sale may come through when, in fact, you've already lost. You may well find that your prospect is including you — letting you think you're at least in contention — merely to satisfy a three-bid requirement, having decided long before to do business with another bidder. If you've learned to assess the sales opportunity with staunch objectivity, you will see through a prospect's friendly façade, seek the truth about the competition, and ascertain whether a deal is possible.

Short of psychotherapy, how would you, as a sales professional, ascertain how objectively you see yourself, your skills, and your capabilities? You'd be lucky to have a capable manager, colleague, or mentor who could help you conduct regular "sanity checks."

Some of my clients use assessment tools to determine traits and expected behaviors of sales job candidates and

---

TACTIC: Over a two-month period, ask several trusted friends, partners, colleagues, or mentors to give you their objective and candid observations on your behaviors and other professional issues. You have to be willing to hear the truth and to make necessary adjustments in the way you see things.

---

team members. You can learn more about these on the web at www.HowWinnersSell.com.

As you read more in this book about the skills, personal traits, and behaviors of winners, try to be objective about yourself. If you find yourself saying, "I know that," or "I do that already," stop and ask yourself for hard evidence. See just how objective you can be.

ESCAPING FROM THE COMFORT ZONE

So — when you do identify a skill or behavior that needs improvement, just how capable of change are you?

A few years ago I was facing two big changes in my life. I was approaching the fiftieth anniversary of my birth, and within a week of that milestone I was going to leave the corporate world for the third time in my career and start The Stein Advantage. I was definitely planning to venture out of two of my comfort zones around the same time.

Needless to say, I was apprehensive. However, being someone who loves and even thrives on change, I decided on a proactive approach. I would go skydiving.

Here's the way I saw it: If I could stand in an open airplane doorway two and a half miles above the ground and will myself to step off into empty space, then I could do anything. If I could do something so counterintuitive, I could meet any challenge. Turning fifty and starting a new business would be a piece of cake.

With this in my mind, I jumped out of my comfort zone. I left the security of a functioning aircraft and entrusted my life to a thin canopy of nylon.

I jumped out of my comfort zone. I resigned my position at the last company where I would ever be an employee.

I jumped out of my comfort zone and started my third company, The Stein Advantage.

I jumped out of my comfort zone and became an expert in enterprise software and services, as well as a "thought leader" to my clients.

I jumped out of my comfort zone and withdrew my first proposal to a client — with no other business in the pipeline — because discounting my services was against my principles.

I jumped out of my comfort zone and celebrated my fiftieth — my best birthday ever — willing to take on anything and everything a person half a century old would have to face.

I jumped out of my comfort zone — and, in doing so, expanded it.

Do you know the boundaries of your comfort zones? Are they real limitations, or merely self-limiting beliefs? If you're putting up your own boundaries, please understand that expanding your comfort zone requires, by definition, discomfort.

I encourage you, for the sake of your professional growth, to invite discomfort occasionally. As winners will tell you, you have only three real options for change:

▶ you can anchor yourself in your comfort zone and be left behind,

▶ you can reluctantly allow yourself to get pulled out of your comfort zone and be somewhat effective some of the time, or

▶ you can take the initiative, expand your comfort zone, and control your professional destiny.

NEW BEHAVIORS

Here are some business-oriented behaviors you might consider to be outside your comfort zone and therefore worth the risk of trying:

▶ Deliver a speech at an industry or association meeting.

▶ Call a stock analyst who follows your customer's industry and offer him insights into that industry.

▶ Cold call twenty-five CEOs.

▶ Walk away from a sales "opportunity" that's not likely to turn into business.

▶ Understand and memorize your best customer's latest financial statements, then talk to that customer about what you learned.

▶ Commit your sales plan to paper (or disk).

▶ Learn about your prospect's top three products, as well as those of their three key competitors, then talk about what you learned on your next sales call.

▶ Refuse to answer an RFP until you meet with the CFO of that company.

▶ Get your coach in a sales campaign to agree to help you win the deal.

▶ Invite your company's CEO to breakfast and pitch to him a logical, well-researched strategy to achieve a corporate goal.

TACTIC: Figure out what enables you to proactively change your behavior. Make an honest, objective appraisal of your attitude toward change, your comfort zones, where you need to be, and what you need to do to get there.

Chapter  3

Take Inventory, Then Stock Up

> **STRATEGY #3. GET INTO SHAPE FOR SELLING "BIGGER"**

Once you are capable (with or without help) of performing an objective self-assessment, you can dig into the skills, attitudes, and behaviors (SABs) you'll need to gain the selling advantage. Because it is ultimately the customers who determine what SABs you need in order to get them to buy from you, each sales position is unique.

43

However, there are some universal SABs that all sales professionals need to develop and maintain. I have grouped these into four broad areas: business know-how, expanding your perspective, communication skills, and competitiveness. We'll go into each of these over the next several chapters.

Let's take a look at key substrategies that will help you develop the skills you need to become a winner.

MAKE SELF-EDUCATION A HABIT

Much of what *How Winners Sell* is all about is knowing more about your customer, client, or prospect than your competition and using that information to your advantage. Information is an asset. You can squander it or invest it for the highest return.

If you're not in the habit of staying on top of news, trends, the opinions of experts, and what is in the best interests of your clients and customers, you need to get there. If you are lucky enough to work for one of the few really advanced, fast corporations that provide this kind of timely information to their sales organizations, you're ahead of the rest. If not, you have to take the responsibility for self-education.

Top sales professionals understand that most of this research into their client's industry has to be done through trade publications, business periodicals, and the Internet. Subscribing to (and reading!) these sources is a good use of your time.

There are four categories of magazines and websites that a sales professional should regularly peruse:

▶ "Business savvy" publications like the *Wall Street Journal, Fortune, Forbes,* and *BusinessWeek.* All those magazines have websites.

"Excellence is a habit, not an event."

— NIDO QUBEIN

- ▶ Technology-oriented business magazines and web-sites, which will give you insights into leveraging information and technology for sales advantage. Examples are *Business 2.0* and *Red Herring.*

- ▶ Industry trade publications — magazines published specifically for people working in (and selling to) those industries, such as *Baking Management, Air Transport World,* and *American Inkmaker.*

- ▶ Magazines and related websites targeting sales professionals and their management. Examples: *SellingPower, Sales and Marketing Management.*

Make sure you know what new business books execu-tives are reading. I won a deal by asking a VP what book he might have seen on the CEO's desk. He told me. I bought

---

TACTIC: Subscribe to and read at least one magazine per category. You can spend weeks trying to get a meeting with an executive, then lose credibility instantly if she tests you by asking your opinion about something you should be familiar with but aren't.

---

and read the book before my meeting with that executive. The CEO and I discussed it, and from that point on, I could do no wrong.

TACTIC: Test yourself. Can you talk for more than ten minutes about current trends or opportunities in each of the four kinds of information I listed above (generic business, business technology, your industry, and sales)? If not, you probably need to spend a bit more of your time reading.

Here's one theme you'll find throughout this book: Know more about your prospect than your competitor does. The more you can help your prospect achieve his business plan, the more likely you are to win the sale.

DEVELOP YOUR OWN RESEARCH TOOLS

If the Internet has done anything for us as sales professionals, it has given us the ability to learn more about our prospects, clients, and customers. Of course, it has done the same for our competitors — so, with the same information available to everyone, how can we gain competitive advantage?

Although publicly held corporations are easy to research, information on private companies is harder to come by. You'll need to get very proficient with your personal computer, PDA, or web-enabled cell phone to quickly find what you need to know.

Here are some tips for finding the information you need on the Internet:

▶ Find a few search engines you can get comfortable with, and learn how to use them, including the advanced features. I currently use several: www.altavista.com, www.google.com, and www.alltheweb.com; for periodicals, I go to www.northernlight.com. At www.ceoexpress.com you'll find a list of the best search engines.

▶ Find alternative sources of information about your clients, customers, and competitors; for example, job-search sites that might indicate new development initiatives, investor bulletin boards (such as those on finance.yahoo.com), and local newspapers where remote sites or plants may be situated.

▶ If you're selling to larger, multinational corporations, especially during times of geopolitical unrest, you need at least a basic understanding of what the experts are saying. Merrill Lynch has a regularly updated document, "Global Economic Trends," that you can download for free at www.ml.com.

▶ Get the fastest connection you can. Period. If you work from a home office, invest in cable modem, DSL, or another broadband solution. If you're on a business trip and will be spending more than fifteen minutes online, pay the nominal fee for a superfast connection to the Internet, if available.

▶ Force yourself not to surf when you should be researching.

▶ Don't believe everything you see on the Internet. Financial statements are generally truthful, but your prospect's website may contain more hype than reality.

▶ Save, bookmark, or print out anything you think may prove valuable. Today's tantalizing, powerful article often becomes the object of tomorrow's two-hour search.

Finally, please understand that some of your favorite and most effective research tools today will be old news tomorrow. Make sure you stay current on the best ways to identify, gather, and analyze the information that's most critical to your job. Regularly monitor the website for *How Winners Sell* at www.HowWinnersSell.com.

Want to know what information to pull down from the Internet about your prospect? It's all there under Strategy #11, Scrutinize Your Prospect.

SELL HIGHER

If you want to win business consistently and predictably, you have to sell to decision makers. And if you're selling big business solutions for big bucks, these decision makers are high-level executives.

I've been asked many times over the years to deliver speeches, run seminars, and create training programs on how to sell to C-level executives. For a long time I thought the issue was simply getting access. I knew just about every trick in the book, and that's what I taught.

Then, to my surprise, I began to hear complaints from salespeople I had trained six months before that they still could not get executive access. What was I doing wrong?

The problem, I discovered as I dug deeper, was no longer their access to decision makers — it was their access to information. It's become difficult to give your prospects information, insight, and experience they can't get elsewhere.

Typically, a motivated salesperson would ask for and get a meeting. But once he got in, he wouldn't know what to say. He would grow uncomfortable. Perhaps the executive would ask him a tough question and the sales rep would be embarrassed not to have a ready answer. He would grow more and more aware that he had nothing of value for the exec, or if he did, he couldn't get it across convincingly. The exec's attention would wander.

This would soon become a self-reinforcing syndrome — one that is perhaps familiar to you. Your meeting with the top executive doesn't go well. A few days later, you call to get another appointment, but he's suddenly unavailable. With growing anxiety, you try to arrange meetings with other high-level executives in this and other companies, and when you have trouble getting in, it doesn't surprise you. You don't pursue them, because even though you're disappointed, the terror of getting in and then not knowing what to say is worse.

How do you avoid falling into this vicious cycle? By becoming more resourceful. I now coach sales reps to work closely with others who can bring value to the prospect's executives: experts from the prospect's company, client base, or noncompeting business partners. Top sales pros these days are veritable brokers of people, resources, and information — the other form of tender.

If you're approaching a new prospect but have not been referred by someone the decision maker trusts, you'll have to earn mindshare with that executive. Make yourself the indispensable broker of information, insight, and expert resources — beyond what the executive can get online, beyond what his company can provide, beyond what your competitor can deliver. This is a proven path to executive-level sponsorship.

> If you're approaching a new prospect but have not been referred by someone the decision maker trusts, you'll have to earn mindshare with that executive. Make yourself the indispensable broker of information, insight, and expert resources.

ASSESSING YOUR ACCESS

Take this little test, based upon what I refer to as Toole's Model (after the seasoned sales executive Gary Toole, who first showed it to me). It will give you a clear picture of where you've been spending your time in an account.

Start with the most important opportunity you're now working on. Down the first column of the chart, write the names of all the key executives, managers, and operations-level people who will be involved in the evaluation, decision, and approval of your offering, ranked from most important to least. Include everyone whose support you will need to win the business.

Across the top, fill in the months or other time divisions appropriate to the length of the evaluation.

Mark the squares to indicate with whom and in which months you've had at least one significant face-to-face meeting, phone call, or discussion. ("Significant" means relating to your contact's issues, opportunities, or challenges, and your contribution toward his or her success.)

Your chart should look something like this:

	Jan	Feb	Mar	Apr	May	Jun	Jul	Aug	Sep
Fred Jones (CEO)	★		★	★		★		★	
Jane So (CFO)	★	★	★		★	★		★	
Luis Garcia (SVP West)	★			★		★			★
Ron Kumar (VP Mfg)	★		★		★		★		
Ira Goldfarb (Cust Svc Mgr)		★		★		★	★	★	★
Jim Flavin (Purchasing Mgr)	★		★	★		★		★	★
Ian Markham (Project Leader)	★	★	★	★	★	★	★	★	★
Cathy Bemis (Accountant)	★	★	★	★	★	★	★	★	★

Some of you will find that your version of Toole's Model looks more like this:

	Jan	Feb	Mar	Apr	May	Jun	Jul	Aug	Sep
Fred Jones (CEO)	★		★						
Jane So (CFO)	★	★	★		★				
Luis Garcia (SVP West)						(vast emptiness)			
Ron Kumar (VP Mfg)	★		★		★				
Ira Goldfarb (Cust Svc Mgr)		★		★		★	★		
Jim Flavin (Purchasing Mgr)	★		★	★		★		★	★
Ian Markham (Project Leader)	★	★	★	★	★	★	★	★	★
Cathy Bemis (Accountant)	★	★	★	★	★	★	★	★	★

If your chart looks like the second one, gaining or main-taining executive access may be out of your comfort zone. You need to explore why this is true, and what you need to do about it.

TACTIC: If you're preparing to call on an executive, have enough informa-tion, insight, and opinion to be able to talk about her world for fifteen minutes longer than the time scheduled for the meeting. If you do this, you will never fear running out of something valuable to say.

BROADEN YOUR AUDIENCE

Business-to-business selling now involves a broader base of interested executives than ever before, often including the board of directors. There is a phenomenon I call "Manage-ment by Magazine." A board member on an airplane reads in an in-flight magazine about some new trend, product, or service. She tears out the article and faxes it to the company's CEO with a note attached: "What are we doing about this?" The CEO is told to add an agenda item to the next board meeting. The CEO scrambles to get educated.

If you're a trusted resource for that CEO, you may wind up getting invited to the board meeting. This is where you can hit the jackpot — or lose it all. Be prepared, if called upon, to talk knowledgeably to anyone who asks a question. For instance, you may feel comfortable selling to the vice president of research and development, but can you convincingly answer a question posed by a marketing executive?

TACTIC: Find out who else in the company might support an investment in your product or service. Perhaps the VP of development favors an initiative that can be funded with the savings from your inventory control system, energy-efficient lighting, or economical delivery trucks. Getting that VP involved in the decision could help you close the deal.

EXCEED EXPECTATIONS

Today, an important part of the value your customer receives has to come not from your company's products or services but from you. Why? Because, chances are, your product or service is not that different from your competitor's. There are too many products, too much hype, too little differentiation, too much discounting — and not enough emphasis on the sales rep.

When your competitor hypes some feature or function of its product or service as its unique selling point, be ready to counter with your own unique selling point — yourself. If you can give your prospect the benefit of your knowledge, experience, insight, contacts, resources, friendship, integrity, an outside perspective, a collaborative vision, a strategy for getting things done, you will have the advantage.

I currently consult for a company that delivers business process reengineering services to the auto industry. One of the company's senior project managers was working with a client who was transferring a Japanese production line to be installed in a domestic plant. Aware that there were critical deadlines, the project manager gave his client the names of electrical and plumbing contractors he had worked with and knew would get the job done on time and on budget. The manufacturer used his recommendations. That's value.

TACTIC: Take the time to figure out what added value you can provide to your clients, customers, or prospects above and beyond your company's products and services. Start with a broad definition; later, get more specific for each customer or customer type.

Exhibit an Executive Demeanor

The people who are most successful at selling to executives are other executives. You may have experienced this yourself: Near the end of a big deal, your boss, or even your company's president, meets with his counterpart in the prospect's company and closes the deal you spent months developing. You're more than a little uncomfortable. You're the one who did most of the work, and now your boss is taking an ego trip at your expense.

But even if you aren't a top executive, you can still act like one. What will persuade a top exec that you have the right stuff? One thing is your ability to understand the world from an executive's perspective, to see the big picture from 40,000 feet. Another key is your ability to command respect.

In the business world, that respect comes from a number of behaviors and traits. These include your general business knowledge, your knowledge of the company and industry, your personal style, your communication skills, your integrity, your ability to drive change toward a vision, your courage, your network of business associates, your ability to manage and maintain relationships, your personal financial success, your analytical ability, and many other positives that may be less obvious.

How can you develop these behaviors? The surest way to learn to act like an executive is simply to *be* one — to make decisions, be accountable for the success or failure of your department, be responsible for the careers and livelihoods of those who work for you. For most sales professionals, of course, this is not possible — and few executives would expect every sales rep to be a former CEO.

However, there are tactics you can use that will give you a foundation on which you can build your executive demeanor. Among them.

▶ Read some books on executive-level topics and thought processes. You can learn how CEOs think, make decisions, and lead, and what is important to them from a business perspective. For a list of current books, go to the resources page at www.HowWinnersSell.com.

▶ Join one or more trade associations for the industry you're selling to. Attend their meetings and conferences. Volunteer to sit on their board. Although many trade shows attract operations-level people, you can find executives speaking at key events.

▶ Regularly read executive-focused magazines such as *Fortune, Forbes, Chief Executive,* and *CFO.* Give *BusinessWeek* a try. If it applies to what you're selling, read *CIO.* Unless your job specifically requires them, stay away from the pure technology magazines. They rarely give you a broad, executive view of anything.

▶ Get out of your comfort zone: ask key executives of your own company for their perspective on the markets you're selling to. What are the most strategic deals they've been involved with? What issues were they able to address?

▶ Whenever you're around executives, listen, observe, and above all, keep an open mind. What valuable skills do they have? Emulate their skills and behaviors as well as you can — listening skills, questioning skills, decision-making skills, and simple decisiveness.

▶ Be sure you look the part as well. Few sales professionals win multimillion-dollar deals without looking as though it's an everyday thing for them. Emulate not only their style but the quality of what they wear, what they drive, even down to what they use to take notes.

▶ Above all, remember that everyone is an individual with a distinctive personal style. Don't assume every executive behaves like the few you've met.

Becoming a winner means investing a lot of time in personal development. The winners consider this investment a necessity, not a luxury. Where do they get the time to do this? From the time they save by not pursuing business they can't or don't want to win.

I will explore this subject in chapter 10.

> "I like thinking big. If you are going to be thinking anything, you might as well think big."
>
> — Donald Trump

Chapter  4

"Let Me See If I Understand . . ."

▶ **STRATEGY #4. ENHANCE YOUR COMMUNICATION SKILLS**

Information is now, more than ever, barter, but time has always been money. It's even more valuable in today's hurry-up, meet-Wall-Street's-expectations business environment. And top executives put a higher premium on their time than anybody.

When you try to contact these decision makers, will they follow up with you themselves, or will they hand you off to their subordinates, or even ignore you? It depends on how effectively you communicate. In this electronic and ostensibly paperless age, this means e-mail and voice mail. How good are yours?

The quality of your communication reflects both your competence as an industry expert and your ability to apply that competence in the service of business goals. Since the difference between winning and losing in our world is often you, the sales professional, and not the product or service you sell, you must show by your communication that you are the person to deal with.

> The quality of your communication reflects both your competence as an industry expert and your ability to apply that competence in the service of business goals.

One thing I consistently hear from educators is how the speaking and writing skills of college students are in a downward spiral. College professors are appalled at the percentage of students, including graduate students, who cannot write more than one grammatically correct sentence in five.

For sales professionals seeking to influence executive-level decision makers, poor communication skills can be fatal. More often than not, the men and women at the top have excellent communication skills and will judge you negatively when they see that yours are deficient. No matter how competent you are, no matter how well you sell to lower-level managers, you are forever pigeonholed by top executives as beneath their notice.

GETTING YOUR MESSAGE ACROSS

The Internet has brought a new age of casual, often sloppy messaging. It's easy for sales professionals to believe that

> *"To listen well is as powerful a means of communication and influence as to talk well."*
>
> — CHIEF JUSTICE JOHN MARSHALL

they can be just as lax in communicating with prospects. This is a fallacy. Although it's true that e-mail is, by its very nature, more casual, good grammar and writing skills are still important. Your messages must be clear and unambiguous. If you can't get your ideas across correctly and concisely, no one will waste time trying to decipher them.

Here are some ways to increase the effectiveness of your e-mail communication with customers and clients:

▶ Ask executives how they like to communicate. Some prefer e-mail. Others detest it. They will appreciate your asking.

▶ Send business contacts unsolicited messages only if they offer obvious value: industry information, competitive insights, new offerings, updates on how you've helped other clients.

▶ Learn to write subject lines that are compelling and concise. Here are a few examples:

Subject: LosingMoney.com predicts lower than expected earnings

Subject: Response to your question about availability of Mike Jones

Subject: Call w/ Sylvia Jackson confirmed. 3/14 2:00 EDT. She will call you.

Reread your e-mails (and use your spell-checker) before you send them. It's important to be understood, but even more important not to be misunderstood.

Even with the rise of e-mail, we still use phones. Whether you like it or not, you'll often find yourself talking to someone's voice mail. Busy executives get a lot of it; whether they decide to answer yours depends on how compelling it is. Sales winners know how to leave messages that are clear, concise, and to the point. Think out your message before you call; be ready for the beep. But don't memorize it or read it, or you'll sound mechanical.

E-mail and voice mail, despite their ease and utility, are not direct communication. They're more like slipping a note under someone's door. In fact, salespeople sometimes use them to avoid direct contact. You call and leave a message when you know your contact isn't at his desk — or, rather than risk calling, you send e-mail. Maybe you don't want to get caught off guard with questions you can't or don't want to answer; maybe you're not comfortable delivering bad news; maybe you simply don't want to spend time on the phone. Whatever your reasons, such one-way communication will keep you from developing the person-to-person relationships you need to be a sales winner. Push out of your comfort zone; strive for person-to-person communication wherever possible.

See Strategy #15 for more on this subject.

DEVELOPING YOUR COMMUNICATION SKILLS

How can you improve your written communication skills? If you are self-motivated and capable of establishing new habits, read a book or two about how to improve your writing. Then practice your skills while writing to friends and associates (on noncritical issues), and follow up to check understanding.

TACTIC: To improve your writing skills, take a business writing course, such as the one offered by the American Management Association.

Many companies and consultants coach sales teams on how to improve their speaking skills and make their presentations more effective. Your company's best interests may be served by using coaches to train your salespeople.

Communication is a cultural behavior, and it varies from place to place. If you're doing business internationally or selling to domestic managers of foreign-owned companies, you need to know at least the basics of their culture. Having done business all over the world, I can tell you that a little knowledge goes a long way. For example, you may be able to differentiate yourself from the competition to a Japanese businessperson just by the way you receive his business

> **TACTIC:** To improve your oral communication skills, join Toastmasters International. Even professional speakers routinely praise that organization and the improvement its members enjoy.

card. (I accept his card with two hands, read both sides, then nod my head. This seems to work well.)

It's important to look objectively at all your communication skills. If you're not sure how well you speak or write, ask someone who knows and is willing to be brutally honest. If you come up short, do something about it. Now.

Become Proficient at Questioning

Internationally known performance consultant Anthony Robbins has some powerful things to say about questions. He contends that you can move forward in your life by simply changing the kind of questions you ask yourself. Don't ask, "How come my job stinks and I never have any money?" Ask, "What can I do today that will work toward changing my employment situation and earning the money I believe I deserve?" I can tell you that this simple shift in approach can change what you accomplish in your day — not to mention your life.

It is the questions you ask yourself that drive your ultimate success as a sales professional. Here are some tough, basic questions that, if asked and answered, will give you

> *"The art and science of asking questions is the source of all knowledge."*
>
> — Adolf Berle

insight, if not motivation, to find the path, stay the course, and do what it takes to achieve sales superiority:

▶ What obstacles are keeping me from setting specific goals for myself, both professionally and personally? What can I do today to list, then overcome, those obstacles?

▶ What obstacles are preventing me from planning and formalizing those plans? What can I do today to list, then overcome, those obstacles?

▶ What strengths can I leverage to make myself more effective as a sales professional? How will I do that, and by when?

▶ What professional weaknesses are keeping me from achieving my goals and objectives? What will happen when I eliminate or compensate for those weaknesses? How, specifically, will I accomplish that, and by when?

It is the answers you get from your client that tell you how well your selling effort is doing. You've probably heard the expression, "You have two ears and one mouth. That means you should listen twice as much as you talk." Jim Meisenheimer puts it differently. He says, "Your ears will outearn your mouth." Top sales professionals have developed advanced skills in asking prospects questions. Every question has a purpose, whether it is to get information, demonstrate understanding, or build personal rapport. Before every phone call or meeting, they know exactly what information they need in order to advance the sales campaign, and what questions will get the right answers.

See chapter 11.

You'll see how important this skill is when we cover qualification (chapter 9) and triage (chapter 10).

ASK, AND KEEP ASKING

Winners seek the truth; they ask themselves questions in pursuit of essential information. Early in the qualification process, for instance, a key question is "Does this prospect have money to invest in my offering?" The top pros find people who can answer this question, as well as independent evidence that the answers they get are correct. They ask the question over and over until they are sure of the truth. If the answer is no, they consider relegating the deal to the back burner until things change. If yes, they keep asking to make sure nothing changes.

A single question asked three times can force you to reassess your progress in a sales campaign. When I consult with a company to help it win a sales opportunity, I always ask the sales rep, "If you just now learned that you lost this deal, what would be the reason?" When she tells me, I ask, "And if that weren't the reason, what would be next?" When she answers that, I ask her the same question for the third time. By then, if she is objective and honest with herself, the reasons she could lose the sale are on the table.

There are other high-level questions you should ask yourself as you pursue business. One of the best is "From the prospect's perspective, why should they buy from me?" When you know the answer to that one, ask, "Why else?"

When it comes to competition, you might ask yourself, "If a new competitor were to drop into this deal right now and jeopardize my position, who would it be?" Next, "What would they do and say?" Then, logically, "How would I prevent them from making any progress?"

Questions work in reverse as well. A consistent winner I occasionally have the pleasure of working with told me, "One of the ways I qualify prospects is by the questions

---

TACTIC: List five questions you will ask yourself each day, the answers to which will help you advance your portfolio of sales opportunities. While you're at it, do the same regarding your professional development.

---

they ask me. I discern their level of competence almost immediately. If the questions are simple or naïve, I know one of two things: either they are new at evaluating solutions like mine and I'm going to spend some time educating them, or I'm going to find that they are not competent to use my solution effectively and I must provide plenty of help, or in the worst case, find another prospect."

Finally, take the perspective of a businessperson. Ask yourself one question: "If I were an executive in my prospect's company — responsible for large sums of money and hundreds or thousands of jobs and careers, knowing what I know about that business and that industry and the competition — would I be persuaded by someone like me?"

This is a big-picture question. To answer it properly, you have to be more than a salesperson; you have to be a businessperson. That's what the next chapter is all about.

Chapter **5**

The Business of Selling

▶ STRATEGY #5. TRANSFORM YOURSELF FROM A SALESPERSON INTO A BUSINESSPERSON

If I told you that one of the most important parts of retooling yourself was *not* to be a salesperson, would you think you picked up the wrong book? Well, I have a good reason for saying it.

But I'm not really saying you shouldn't be a salesperson. I'm saying that to be a top sales professional, you have to be a businessperson — because businesspeople make the most effective salespeople. And why is that true? Because — repeat after me — it's all about money.

I feel so strongly about this that I figured it deserved its own strategy. As you can see.

In terms of selling, what do I mean by "businessperson"? A businessperson is someone who can transcend the product or service she is selling to reach higher ground — the ability to understand, articulate, and drive the contribution her business can make to the client's business.

What is the business value of your product or service? To communicate this to your prospect convincingly, you must be more than a sales rep. You have to be a businessperson and, using business competencies, view and present your offering as a medium for delivering business value. As SAMA's Lisa Napolitano put it, "At the top of the playing field, you are talking about a business manager."

Being a businessperson not only means demonstrating the skills I described in the introduction to this part, such as the ability to read a financial statement, it also involves a way of thinking and being. Here are some of the behaviors and traits I have observed in sales winners — people I would also consider businesspeople:

▶ They know that if they give their customer what he needs, they will then get what they need.

▶ They make rational decisions, rather than allowing emotion to guide them.

▶ They follow orderly procedures and processes, rather than taking random actions.

> *"It's not the strongest of the species that will survive, nor the most intelligent, but the ones most responsive to change."*
> — Charles Darwin

- ▶ They plan for the future and have the discipline and motivation to execute that plan.

- ▶ They seek out the truth through insightful, probing questions, rather than blindly accepting what they are told.

- ▶ They accept responsibility for their own actions and for those who work on their behalf.

- ▶ They know how to use technology to improve not only their own but their customer's business position.

- ▶ They work for a win-win solution, knowing that anything else will ultimately be lose-lose.

If you don't want your client to treat your product or service as a commodity, you have to differentiate your offering from your competitor's. It comes down to perception. If your clients see you as just a salesperson, they won't respect you the way they would someone they viewed as a businessperson. Here's how they think: A businessperson is a professional; a businessperson is there for the long haul. Salespeople are all the same, interchangeable; they're just after a quick buck. This perception, common among top executives, is unfair, but it's a fact of life. That's why people

---

TACTIC: Consider joining the Strategic Account Management Association, whose conferences, journals, and studies provide information and insight on trends, issues, and best practices in strategic and global account management.

---

who sell for a living adopt titles such as Marketing Representative, Business Development Manager, and Client Acquisition Executive on their business cards.

Take a good look at yourself. Read the list of behaviors again. Can you identify areas where you need to improve? What should you do?

First, accept the fact that you, and you alone, are responsible for your own personal and professional growth. No one is going to barge through your door and change you. You've already recognized that a change is needed. That's the toughest step.

MENTORS

Many top sales professionals have had the benefit of a mentor — someone, usually an experienced professional, who gave them a vision of success, along with the strategies and tactics to achieve it. A mentor can serve as a sounding board, help the protégé expand her network, and give honest feedback on progress.

Sales executives may not be the most effective mentors to people who work for them. The demands of their own jobs may make them too subjective, and the appearance of favoritism may cause resentment within the rest of the team. However, a sales professional with five or ten years of experience can probably find mentors within his business network, and perhaps identify what he wants the mentor to help him with as well.

TACTIC: Find someone who exhibits the behavior you want to emulate. If it's someone who's approachable and available to you, consider asking him or her to mentor you through personal or professional changes in that area.

Consider having more than one mentor. There are often many areas in which we need to become more effective; we can use all the help we can get.

Mentoring has to be beneficial for both protégé and mentor. Make sure you know what the mentor expects to gain from mentoring you. When you find a potential mentor, find out how he has benefited from mentoring other people.

EXPAND YOUR GENERAL BUSINESS KNOWLEDGE

How much do you know about business in general? Do you know how businesses operate? What about your company? What about your three best clients? Can you articulate their visions? Can you identify their short- and long-term strategies?

> **TACTIC:** Develop the skill of zooming in and zooming out — looking at your client's company from 40,000 feet, diving deeply into relevant details, only to zoom out to the big picture again.

To survive and thrive in the information economy, the most important skill you'll need is good, old-fashioned business know-how. You should know how businesses operate, especially in your marketplace. Become familiar with concepts and current practices in business strategy and planning, Internet commerce, business collaboration, and change management, among other areas.

One of my clients, bidding to replace a company's decade-old software with a new product that would let independent agents enter orders, asked how the company proposed to get the agents to accept the changeover. There was a stunned silence. Nobody in the company had imagined that the independents might resist the idea. My client, having uncovered an unidentified risk, locked up the deal by adding management services to the proposal.

FINANCIAL STATEMENTS REVISITED

The most important element of business know-how is understanding how financial statements represent a company's financial position and how that company compares with others in its market. If you can't read and interpret an income statement, cash flow statement, or balance sheet, learn to do so right away. There are no shortcuts. Those financial statements are as revealing of business health as CAT scans, EKGs, and blood tests are of your physical health. You don't need to become a CPA, but a solid knowledge of financial concepts and an ability to compare clients are key.

If you believe, as I do, that effective selling at the executive level is about quantifying and proving the business value you can contribute, then having business know-how is a vital component of that approach. If you don't have it, how do you get it? Here are a few ideas:

▶ Take a course in reading and interpreting financial statements at your local college, at night school, or (in the United States) with the American Management Association. In Europe, try Management Centre Europe.

▶ Read a book on the subject. Do the exercises.

▶ Ask your brokerage firm for guides to reading and interpreting financial statements. Most large brokerage houses have either a book or a comprehensive document on the subject.

▶ Spend some time with your own company's CFO, controller, or accountant. If you aren't well versed in finance, do you know someone who can interpret a financial report for you in a pinch?

▶ If you have a close relationship with a client, ask his CFO, controller, or accountant to walk you through the company's financials. This is a very powerful way to understand how your client's business operates. If you sell into a vertical market, this approach will give you real insight into that industry, which can be used when selling to other companies. We're not talking about sharing proprietary information, of course, but industry norms — median profit margins, sales costs, revenues per employee, anything that will help you show how your offering contributes to their business plan.

Remember the timeless truth about sales? That's right: It's all about money. So if you can't show your clients how your offering will earn or save them big money, you'll never consistently win the big sale.

Sell Deep and Rich, Within Your Niche

STRATEGY #6. BECOME AN EXPERT IN THE INDUSTRY INTO WHICH YOU SELL

There is not a doubt in my mind — and evidently not in the minds of the executives running the world's biggest industrial and service companies that sell to other corporations — that a niche or vertical focus wins business.

This vertical-market approach has never been more important than now, when the abundance of companies,

71
△

products, approaches, consultants, solutions, technology, tools, equipment, and services makes differentiation a perpetual, if not impossible, goal.

If you are a salesperson who sells a "horizontal" product or service, such as generic management consulting, call-center hardware and software technology, or fleets of general utility trucks — anything sold across multiple industries — please consider verticalizing. If your company won't support that approach, you might consider approaching your territory vertically, by industry, focusing on only one or two, at least for the time being. On the surface, it may seem that this would limit your prospects and therefore constrain how much you could sell; but by the end of this chapter, I'm sure you'll see why I recommend this approach.

The chart below shows four basic approaches to becoming knowledgeable about prospective buyers. The wishful

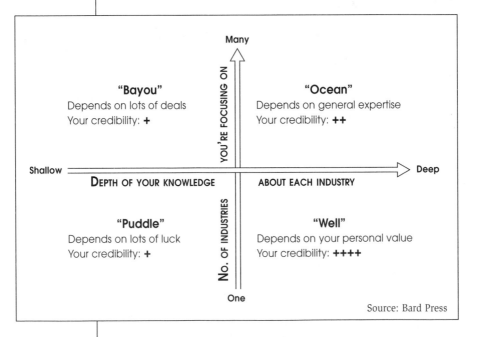

Source: Bard Press

thinkers, of course, are those in the "puddle" quadrant, knowing very little about a very few industries. They depend on luck, rather than focused expertise, to win business.

To many, the "bayou," where you know a little bit about a lot of industries, is alluring; what's better than having potential clients in any industry? "After all, if only 10 percent buy, I'm still in great shape, right?" Sure, if you don't mind wasting 90 percent of your effort on unpaid work.

Others like selling to the "ocean." They believe they can sell anything to anyone, that being a generic expert will save the day. But they are unable to generate much credibility in any industry because of the time and effort it would take to achieve expert status in all.

I recommend concentrating your attentions on the "well," where your selling effort, like your knowledge, is deep, narrow, focused, and bubbling with credibility.

SELLING IN THE WELL

A sales professional should focus on a single industry and become an expert in it. Why? Because executive-level buyers with big challenges want proven solutions from experts who understand, not from generalists. Suppose you broke your leg in seven places in a skiing accident. Would you go to your family doctor, a general practitioner? Unlikely. You'd consult the best orthopedic surgeon you could find, one who has successfully repaired fifty or more injuries like yours.

What does being an expert in one industry get you?

A network of business contacts. When you sell to colleges on Monday, the government on Tuesday, and furniture manufacturers on Wednesday, it's hard to develop critical mass in your business network. Once you focus on a single industry, however, it's amazing how one contact seems to know many others, all with at least one important common interest — the industry.

"The successful man is the average man, focused."

— ANONYMOUS

New opportunities. When moving from job to job, executives tend to stay in the same industry. So do other management-level employees. Those contacts, as they move from company to company, can open new doors for you at high levels and provide the political leverage you need to win a competitive sales opportunity.

Visibility. When you join your target industry's trade or professional organization and regularly attend meetings, your face, your name, and your company's name become familiar to the other members. This visibility and recognition generates leads, and it can bring you an introduction to or consideration from someone who may be looking to buy what you're selling.

Information. Knowledge gives you power, and knowledge comes from information. Your credibility with an executive depends in large part on how much you know about his industry. When you're focusing on a single industry, you can develop sources of information that will help you outsell your competition. You know what the industry and security analysts are saying about your client, its competitors, and the future of the industry. You subscribe to trade magazines and focus your web surfing on what's happening in that market. You immerse yourself in information, and if you know how and when to use it, you have the inside track.

History. When you've focused entirely on one industry for a while, you'll understand its history — in fact, you will have lived it. You know which companies thrived, which failed, who the key players were, the stories and the legends. This bolsters your credibility with executives in that industry.

Knowledge of critical business issues. I'm amazed at how marketing executives scream and holler when buyers commoditize their products and services, yet do nothing to create business and industry-specific value that would, if properly marketed and sold, keep that from happening. Knowing the business challenges and opportunities and being able to discuss them, in industry terms, at an executive level — that's a powerful credibility builder and differentiator.

A vision of the future. Once you've sold into an industry for several years, you start to see how global events and economic trends affect your customers. There comes a time when you can begin to extrapolate what has happened into what's likely to happen. When you can position your product or service as part of your customer's vision of the future, you're on your way to a sale, and probably one with less price sensitivity.

References. One of the most important benefits of selling within a single industry is the ability to provide personal and business references your prospect will instantly recognize. When you can rattle off names of executives your prospect knows personally, who will vouch for your integrity and your ability to get the job done as promised, you'll find yourself with competitive advantage.

Selling vertically within a single industry is all about building credibility. There are few things as effective in advancing a sales campaign as getting in front of an executive

See Strategy #21 for more about building references.

TACTIC: How do you become an expert in an industry? Immerse yourself. Read all you can. Join the associations and become an active, contributing member. Regularly check websites that specialize in providing information by industry. Visit www.HowWinnersSell.com. Talk to all your clients and customers about their current and future challenges and opportunities. Read industry analysts' reports. Compare and contrast the main competitors in that industry. Gather enough information to make a prediction (perhaps you should keep the first one to yourself!). Watch the stock prices. Read press releases of the key players. See where they are going and how they intend to get there. Understand what issues they're addressing. Live in that world.

---

and earning instant credibility. Of the many things that a sales professional can do to earn that credibility, being an expert in the prospect's industry is near the top.

One other thing: when you become an industry expert, you understand the nuances well enough to propose exactly what your client needs in order to achieve its objective. No guesswork. No fluff. Just like that world-class orthopedic surgeon who fixed up your leg.

As you continue to deliver what you promise to businesses in your chosen industry, your critical mass will build, more opportunities will present themselves, and you will win more often.

"If It Weren't for the Competition..."

► STRATEGY #7. GET INTO A COMPETITIVE STATE OF MIND

Who are your competitors, and what are they doing right now to take your customers away? If you can't answer these questions day after day, your livelihood is at risk. What you don't know about your competition can hurt you — badly. This chapter will tell you how to get in the habit of being constantly aware of your competitors and alert to their activities.

77
△

Once you get to know your competitors — not just the companies and their products or services, but the habits of each salesperson you'll be going up against — you can begin to base your strategies and tactics on that knowledge. And if you stay up to date, you can outsell your competitor today, tomorrow, and next year.

One of my client accounts is an information technology consulting firm. They are very, very good at what they do, and they are small. (Notice I didn't say "but.") When they compete against the big guys, their size is always brought up as an issue. They have learned to immunize their clients against this concern.

When they present themselves to a prospect, they begin by talking about the many advantages of doing business with a focused, specialized, lean organization. Then they predict, subtly and professionally, that their competition will try to portray their size as a handicap, rather than the strength it really is.

This is offense, not defense; it's a trap. When the big companies try, as expected, to exploit my client's size, the prospect quickly dismisses that issue, leaving the attacker in a very uncomfortable position.

THIRD PLACE GOES TO . . .

It's been said again and again that sales is a zero-sum game. If you're going to win, someone else must lose. There's no second place.

To drive the point home, I often joke with participants at my seminars, "Today we are going to announce the winner of the contract for outsourcing our entire IT capability. For their incredibly creative job on the RFP, the third prize

> "Some people are so far behind in the race, they believe they are leading."
> — UNCLE JUNIOR, A CHARACTER IN THE SOPRANOS (HBO TV)

This is the first of two chapters on competition. Later, in chapter 17, we'll dig into the types of competitive knowledge you'll need in order to outsell your competition.

of $100,000 goes to Hi-Tek Corporation. That should cover your basic cost of sales, ladies and gentlemen. Here's your check — and thanks!

"The company that takes second prize, blowing away everyone on the evaluation team with a long list of satisfied references, is — Wow-Em-All-The-Time-Co. We are pleased to award you $200,000. That will cover your expenses and give all the members of your sales team a nice little bonus.

"And finally, the winner of the five-year, $37 million contract is. . . ." Ah, wouldn't that be nice.

But it doesn't work that way. One company wins the deal, and everyone else loses, with nothing to show for it but bruised egos, expense reports to fill out, a dismal quarter or year, and perhaps even lost momentum in the marketplace. A few heads may roll, too.

I was a teenager growing up in the Bronx in the early 1960s. Life was tough. I had several bikes stolen, one by a gang of toughs who took it from me by force. I was repeatedly jumped by complete strangers in the streets and beaten up in the schoolyard for no apparent reason. When I got old enough to drive, I earned a little money and bought what turned out to be a series of used cars. Some were broken into, others simply disappeared.

So I grew up, learned karate, went back to my old neighborhood, and got even, right? No, not quite. But I did learn to fight. When you grow up looking over your shoulder all the time, you learn a lot about protecting your turf, if not your physical safety. It made me very competitive, careful about keeping tabs on people who would be very happy to take business from me, ethically or not. I have leveraged that skill into my business.

ETHICS

Let's talk a bit about ethics. When I begin working with a sales team, I ask them to picture a square playground with a fence on each side. The fence on the north side stops them from doing anything illegal. The south fence keeps them from violating their employer's rules of engagement. The east fence keeps them from violating common business ethics, and the west fence protects them from violating their own personal principles and values. Do you see what we've done? We have defined the rules.

Staying inside this playground is a good way to keep yourself out of trouble. However, I've found that many sales

---

TACTIC: Since you have competed and will again compete against sales reps with different ethics, decide in advance what you will and will not do. This frees you to be creative, to focus on winning, and to fight hard without compromising your values.

---

professionals spend too much time trying to stay in the exact center of it, fearing perhaps that a big hand will reach over the fence and pull them, kicking and screaming, into territory where they'll commit acts they will later regret.

The Internet has made competition fiercer. Press releases have become a new tool for hyping and positioning, often in ways that can mislead potential buyers, the media, and even industry and securities analysts. Websites are carefully engineered to show vendors in the best possible light. More than ever before, sales professionals are left to fight it out in the field, with ever-diminishing guidance and help from their employers.

> Press releases have become a new tool for hyping and positioning, often in ways that can mislead potential buyers, the media, even industry and securities analysts.

So, in today's world of "hype and snipe" selling, how do you compete effectively against companies that will do anything — and I mean anything — to win a sale? Business-to-business sales professionals, who depend upon personal integrity and the delivery of business value to their customers, face a daunting challenge.

If you've been in sales awhile and achieved a certain level of success, you're probably well aware that in sales, things are not always "fair." But when you're out there in the field, fighting it out every day, you must realize that the only way to compete against someone who doesn't play fairly is to simply outsell him.

What are your weapons in this uneven fight? The strategies and tactics in your sales plan, and your complete understanding of your competitor — not just what he sells, but how he sells it.

Keeping a competitive state of mind carries risks. I've seen salespeople go over the line, lose objectivity, nurse grudges, and let their emotions run their business. But revenge is counterproductive. As Mario Puzo's character Michael Corleone said in *Godfather III*, "Never hate your enemies. It affects your judgment."

AWARENESS

The Internet, as we've said, is a great source of information about our prospect's organization, products, services, customers, future directions, and, in the case of public companies (thanks to the SEC), key strengths and weaknesses.

TACTIC: Go outside your areas of familiarity and observe how people, countries, companies, and teams compete. If you watch football, flip to a Sunday morning talk show and see how liberals and conservatives square off against each other. If you're a student of domestic politics, try following the news about a dispute between two nations. This will help you gain a broader insight into the nature of competition.

But here's the kicker: the Internet is also a window into your competitors. Sales winners realize this; they focus their attention on not only their prospects but their competition.

There are many, many skills and personal traits you need to be a consistently effective sales professional in our hypercompetitive information economy. What we've done here is to highlight and explore a few of these we consider crucial: the objectivity, will, and ability to assess yourself; a business orientation; and a focused approach to dealing with customers and competitors.

To get you into that competitive state of mind, here's a bit of wisdom from Andrew Carnegie: "The first man gets the oyster; the second man gets the shell."

Part

Checking Out the Sales Opportunity

This part covers sales leads and their sources, qualification, and triage. Qualification is the process we use to decide whether to pursue or continue pursuing a sales opportunity. Triage is the act of evaluating opportunities and deciding how much of our effort and resources to spend on each.

At the end of this part of *How Winners Sell*

▶ You will understand the sales lead value ladder and be able to assess more quickly and confidently your chances of winning an opportunity.

▶ You will have a new perspective on qualification and understand how triage can be applied to increase your sales effectiveness.

▶ You will learn exactly what information you need about your prospect to gain competitive advantage.

▶ You will understand the benefits of knowing specifically what your prospect is buying before you begin selling.

"Sorry to have taken your time, Mr. Chiang, but I don't think there's a fit here."

Chapter 8

"Please Respond on or Before . . ."

STRATEGY #8. MOVE UP THE SALES LEAD VALUE LADDER

Salespeople learn of impending sales opportunities in a number of ways. Some leads are temptations disguised as opportunities, as when your company is included in an evaluation only to validate an earlier decision to use your competitor. Others are situations in which, having nurtured an opportunity for years, you have the inside track. Most lie somewhere between these extremes.

85

One way of thinking about different kinds of leads is to see them as a ladder. The lowest rungs are the least desirable leads; what you aspire to are the valuable leads at the top of the ladder.

In the lower right quadrant of the diagram below are the worst of the worst. You've entered the evaluation late and

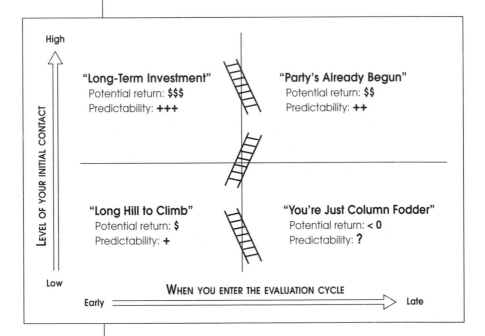

your contacts are at the lowest level of the organization. You can't expect this to turn out well; in fact, you're probably there just to prove someone's case for another vendor.

Up the ladder a few notches (lower left quadrant) is the early lead with low-level contact. You're a little better off than coming in late, but you've still got a long way to go to sign the contract.

> "Opportunity may knock only once, but temptation leans on the doorbell."
>
> — Anonymous

You're doing better if your contacts are at a high level, even if you're entering late. This may happen if the prospect decides none of the other contenders is up to the job and reopens the bidding process. A high-level contact can be like the manager of a baseball team sending in a relief pitcher (you) late in the game.

Best of all is to get into the game early, and at the highest level of access to the company. This takes time, patience, and credibility, but it pays off in a big way. You get to participate in planning, perhaps even write the RFP. You can predict with some certainty when you will get the contract, and for how much.

THE SALES OPPORTUNITY SPECTRUM

Now let's talk about leads in more specific terms. The following list starts with the worst leads and ends with the highest-quality opportunities. It ranges from the type of lead least likely to result in business and finishes with the kind everybody would like to have — the sure thing. When you finish reading, you'll probably remember some past campaigns and realize you were chasing opportunities you had lost even before you showed up.

▶ You check your snail- or e-mail box and find an RFP (request for proposal) or an RFI (request for information). This is usually a bad sign — a signal that the train has left the station and you haven't even bought your ticket. You've probably heard a colleague or sales manager say, "If you haven't written the RFP for or with the prospect, your competitor has, so winning is somewhat less than a remote possibility."

▶ You receive a photocopy of a "bingo card" from a magazine ad your company placed. Before you decide that the quality of such a lead is about as low as you can go, please realize that some sales professionals, due to situations beyond their control, would love to have this kind of lead — in fact, any lead.

▶ You get an e-mail alert from an online service where you've registered your company's products or services. As you become more and more adept at using the Internet to advance your sales and business plans, you'll find new sources every day for potential clients. Come often to www.HowWinnersSell.com for the latest resources.

▶ You receive a form from your internal sales or lead-generation team. Rarely do I find an organization that has created an effective, integrated, closed-loop approach to generating, following up, and closing leads. Many companies just haven't figured out how to do this.

▶ An "independent" consultant, retained by an unnamed company to help them procure a specific product or service, contacts you. If your company has a good history with this consultant, that's good news. Otherwise, you're little more than column fodder, helping the consultant fill out a spreadsheet that will show why you shouldn't be selected.

▶ You get a call from a current customer inviting you to participate in an evaluation. This is bad news: it means you're on your way to losing the account. Once your competitor is in the door, you're on the defensive, which is not a good position to sell from. This happens often — more often than it should. The cause is almost always ineffective account management.

▶ A client drops you a note: one of his customers needs what you sell. Such a lead is often high quality, for two reasons. First, you may get in the door early enough to help the prospect formulate criteria for the buying decision; second, being introduced to an executive by one of his business associates is one of the surest ways to get an appointment, along with instant credibility. Winners make a habit of asking their clients to refer them to others in their business circle. That's a great way to get high-quality leads.

▶ Your personal marketing campaign, aimed at the twenty accounts you want the most, yields a solid lead. Maybe you've been reading Tony Parinello's book, *Selling to VITO,* or using some other highly focused, value-oriented approach to get the attention of high-level industry executives. If so, it worked.

◀ VITO stands for Very Important Top Officer.

▶ Using your knowledge and experience in the industry, you find an unmet need, one either known or unknown by the company, in an existing account. This is high-level action — it's where the top guns, the sales winners who earn a million dollars a year, play. Once you've established yourself as an expert, you can follow your network into companies you've never sold to but where your reputation precedes you.

◀ See Strategy #6.

Now you can see that the farther down the list you progress, the greater the initial investment that's needed to make it happen. A bigger investment, of course, returns a better lead, one with a better chance of turning into business.

RFP GAMES

Have you ever helped a prospect draw up an RFP? It's a wonderful experience. If they do a full evaluation that includes your competitors, you can hear the starting gun go off as you round the first turn.

But if you aren't the one providing the RFP. . . .

TACTIC: Top salespeople know that if they can get into a company before an initiative is officially announced, they have a better chance of getting the inside track. Spend some of your time monitoring press releases, analysts' reports, SEC filings, industry reports, and whatever else you can find about your target industries and accounts, so that if you see an opportunity to make a contribution, you are there first.

Recently I heard from George, an experienced sales professional at one of my client companies, who had inherited the WonderCo (made-up name) account from another sales rep in a territory reassignment. Shortly after making contact with the company, George got a spreadsheet-based RFP from their CIO requesting information: how did George's

89
△

company propose to meet WonderCo's enterprise software requirements for three additional sites?

George immediately became suspicious. "I didn't write the RFP," he thought. "The rep I succeeded didn't write the RFP. He obviously didn't do a good job with WonderCo; otherwise, I wouldn't be in this situation now. But that's water under the bridge.

"The 480 questions in the RFP look just like features of a product that generally does what mine does, but it is clearly not mine. One of my competitors wrote this. That competitor has an ally in WonderCo, and he's going to use my answers as justification for not choosing my product."

George is a top performer, and he had other, more promising leads to pursue and accounts to manage. His instincts told him not to waste valuable time on this bid. But he had a hunch — one that would cost him and his tech expert only a few minutes to check out.

They opened the RFP spreadsheet, went directly to File > Properties > Summary, and found the originator of the requirement list. It was the product marketing department of a competitor's company. There it was, staring out at them from the screen: the smoking gun.

George went straight over the CIO's head to WonderCo's CFO. The CFO said he found it difficult to believe the evaluation was rigged. Several calls and heated discussions later, George decided to withdraw from the competition — one he knew he had little or no chance of winning.

This sort of thing happens every day. When a sales rep receives an RFP that he didn't write, it's a fair bet the competition wrote it, or at least heavily influenced it.

LOOK FOR THE PATTERN

To understand the source and quality of your business, categorize your past three years' wins and losses by lead source. You should begin to see a pattern that can help you reshape your business development approach. For instance, if you find that bingo cards lead only to sporadic deals, you may decide not to waste any more time with leads from that source. You may discover that leads from a regional auditing firm resulted in several lucrative sales; obviously that's a source of leads you need to spend more time and energy on.

Analyze this information and decide whether you are fully leveraging your client relationships, your inside sales capabilities, your partnerships with other suppliers, your marketing campaigns, and, yes, even your somewhat rusty cold-calling skills, if they are appropriate. Figure out what strategies you need, and which supporting tactics, to move up the sales lead value ladder toward higher-quality leads.

Chapter 9

They Evaluate You, You Qualify Them

STRATEGY #9. UNDERSTAND THAT QUALIFICATION IS A PROCESS, NOT AN EVENT

So you have a lead. Now what do you do?

Let's start by understanding the word "qualify." It shares the same root as the word quality — the Latin word *qualis*, "of what kind." Here's where you get to determine what kind of business opportunity you have in front of you.

93
△

Think of it this way: Your prospects get to evaluate you, and you get to qualify them. They can eliminate you at any time, right up to the contract signing. And you can decide, at any time, right up to contract signing, that the quantity and quality of the business they might award you is too small to warrant spending any more of your time, your energy, or your company's money.

Few sales reps see it in those terms. They feel somehow subservient. If the prospect says, "Do a seal-and-penguin show Monday at 8:00 am in our Lapland facility," more than a few reps would be on the phone booking flights with Ice Air.

But you shouldn't look at it that way. It's likely that the business value of the products or services your company delivers, if installed, implemented, and used correctly, will be far greater than the client's investment.

Where does that place you? In a position of strength. From strength comes confidence. Strength and confidence give you the inalienable right to qualify.

Here's an example of an early conversation you might want to have with your prospect. Please don't immediately dismiss it as too aggressive or pushy.

Ms. Prospect, I sincerely appreciate being asked to participate in this evaluation. If you'll give me a minute, I'd like to propose a framework upon which we might work together.

Don't use an exact number unless you know it's accurate.

My company has calculated that participating in a typical evaluation, such as the one you've begun, costs us more than $51,000 in expenses. Now, I understand, of course, that your company is making a large investment in this evaluation as well. However, at the end of this process, you will wind up with a supplier, whereas my company might wind up with nothing.

With that in mind, it's important that I understand not only your business requirements but other aspects of your company and the people who will be involved with this project as well. I need to assure myself that we understand not only what you need and how well we meet those requirements, but also how well we represent our capabilities during the evaluation.

We will certainly abide by any reasonable request from you and your team for information about us, our offering, our approach, and our references. We'll go above and beyond what you ask. In return, I'd like your assurance that you will keep us up to date with the information we need in order to see if it makes sense to keep pursuing your business.

Suppose the executive says, "You're a vendor and we're the customer. You can do what we tell you, or we can find ten other companies to take your place." What should you do? Personally, I'd walk, because the chances are remote that I would ever gain enough control of the evaluation to win the sale.

On the other hand, if the executive's response is in any way positive, here's what you've accomplished:

▶ You've earned the right to ask qualification questions as the evaluation progresses, and you'll probably get useful answers. More important, you've opened the door to probe into areas where your company can provide business value well above that specified in the RFP or brought up during evaluation. The more business value you show them and the more you demonstrate your expertise in their company and industry, the more forthcoming the executives will be with answers that provide more information and insight.

▶ You've established the foundation for a win-win relationship. If you jump whenever the prospect snaps his fingers, what kind of relationship are you training the client to expect after the sale? Sales representatives who have conversations like the one above differentiate themselves immediately from the competition. It takes guts, and it shows that the sales professional is a businessperson, looking out for her company's best interests — which will, in the end, also be the best interests of the customer.

> Caution: There's a fine line between confidence and arrogance. This message must be delivered in a way that reflects not only your personal style but the culture of your company and of your prospect.

> See chapter 15.

95

▶ You've laid the groundwork for earning some control of the buying process later on.

OBJECTIVITY AND VIGILANCE

Back in chapter 2, we looked at the importance of inward-focused objectivity — the will to seek the truth, however uncomfortable, about your own strengths and weaknesses. In a similar way, effective qualification requires outward-focused objectivity that is relentless, detached, and unemotional. You need to know the truth about every sales opportunity, and you need to be vigilant for changes that affect it.

When your doctor is trying to find out what's making you sick, you don't want her to be anything but objective, do you? You want her to ask hard questions — not only those you can answer directly, but also those she can ask by using X-rays, MRIs, and EKGs — to discover what's really going on.

A sales rep needs to know what's happening, too. Not having a way to X-ray the prospect, however, the sales rep must rely mostly on questions. Those questions must produce answers that yield an objective and accurate picture of what's going on.

Not all answers will be objective, of course. With a winner's diagnostic skills, we can examine the answers for inconsistencies: what different people say, what one person says at different times, what people say with different people in the room. We can use our skill at interpreting body language to gain insight into what people are actually thinking when they are telling us what they think we want to hear.

We must also be vigilant. That is, we must keep asking the same questions over and over, of different people and in different settings, and stay alert for answers and behaviors that change over time.

When you are first told of an evaluation, the prospect paints a rosy picture. You are encouraged to submit a proposal, because your participation will give the prospect more choices — or at least proof that the company's three-bid

Read a book on body language. It will change your perceptions of what people really mean when they communicate.

requirement was met. However, it's no secret that your prospect's attitudes and behaviors will change during the evaluation; unless the deal is wired for you to win, they're guaranteed to change. New competitors will be introduced; evaluation team members will come and go; decision criteria will be added, dropped, emphasized, or de-emphasized; funding will be reallocated to or from other projects; mergers or acquisitions will cause priorities to change; decision deadlines will slip; your coach will get reassigned. Any of these can affect your ability to bring in the contract at the time and amount you predicted.

A word to the inexperienced: Be especially careful about getting fixated on your first impressions. If you fail to seek objective information, if you don't stay alert for changing conditions, you will lose the sale long before you are aware of it. If you don't see things as they really are at every moment, you will be fooled by the false attentions of prospects who tell you what you want to hear. You'll pay the price for having "happy ears" — the loss of precious time that you might have used to pursue a genuine opportunity.

A FLIGHT OF INSIGHT

Let me demonstrate the importance of both objectivity and diligence in qualification. Several years ago, while flying my plane home from a strategy session with a client's sales team, I realized that, in many ways, flying is analogous to successfully managing and controlling a sales campaign.

The weather that day was rainy with low clouds. This meant I couldn't fly under visual flight rules (VFR), using ground references. Instead I would have to rely on my instruments for every aspect of the flight. In such conditions, the Federal Aviation Administration requires pilots to file an IFR (instrument flight rules) flight plan. As it happens, I enjoy the challenge of flying under such conditions.

Before long, I was cleared to my destination by air traffic control. I took off and flew along my predetermined route. Since I was in the clouds, unable to see the ground,

I continually scanned the instruments on the control panel, monitoring the performance of the plane, the conditions of flight, and my position at each moment.

As I thought about the elements of my flight plan — departure point, departure time, altitude, route, destination, time en route, amount of fuel on board (in hours), alternate airports, and so forth — I was struck by the parallels to key elements of our sales plan. For an objective evaluation of the conditions of flight and the aircraft, I had to rely solely on my instruments. And to make sure nothing changed without my knowing it, I had to be vigilant, constantly scanning those instruments.

Here I was, staking my life on the same kind of objective measurement and monitoring of conditions a sales winner needs to win a sales campaign. What a revelation!

It turned out to be a fairly routine IFR flight, which gave me the opportunity to further think through these analogies.

Winners develop an ability to monitor sales opportunities the same way a pilot monitors flight conditions — constantly and vigilantly scanning key indicators. They are instantly aware when key qualification criteria change — such as when the project gets suddenly but quietly shuttled to the back burner, or communication with a key person becomes awkward, or a competitor's terminology starts being used.

Depending on instruments means putting your faith in objective measurements. When you're flying a plane, your senses may lie when you lose sight of the ground. Inside a cloud, even experienced pilots get disoriented. You may feel you're turning or diving or climbing even when you're flying straight and level, or that you're flying straight and level when you're actually in a graveyard spiral.

> *"What is that mountain goat doing way up here in the clouds?"*
>
> — PILOT FLYING JETLINER IN A GARY LARSON *FAR SIDE* CARTOON

The Control Panel Analogy

Instrument	Function	Analogy in Qualification
Attitude Indicator	The pilot's primary reference instrument; shows pitch (nose level, up, or down) and roll (wings level or banked)	Attitude of buyers: Are you "climbing" in their view, "descending," or "level"? Are you following your sales plan or being diverted by competition?
Altimeter	The plane's altitude: Are you high enough to clear all obstacles?	Are you selling at a high enough level not to be blocked by lower-level obstacles (gatekeepers)? Are you discussing high-level business issues or meaningless details?
Airspeed Indicator	How fast are you going? If you fly too slow, you'll lose lift and stall.	Are you gaining, losing, or maintaining strength and presence?
Fuel Gauge	How much fuel do you have?	Do you have sufficient resources to sustain your efforts until the deal is won?

But instruments do not lie. If you ignore your senses and emotions and fly strictly by your instruments, you'll come out all right. The same is true when you're qualifying a sales opportunity. Emotionally, you may want to believe it's going well for you, but if you get an objective measurement of your chances, you may find you're heading for a rough landing.

The similarities extend further. The FAA requires that the "pilot in command shall, before beginning a flight, become familiar with all available information concerning that flight." I would propose that "a sales professional in command of an opportunity shall, before beginning a campaign, become familiar with all available information concerning that campaign." The FAA requires pilots to file a flight plan

Section 91.103, Federal Aviation Regulations

99

△

**Details of
sales planning
will be
covered in
chapters 13
and 16.**

for instrument flights; a sales winner plans his sales campaign thoroughly before pursuing a sales opportunity.

QUALIFICATION CRITERIA

Every company has its own qualification criteria for each product or service it markets. Here are some basic criteria that a typical company would apply — not just once, but throughout the selling cycle — to any big sales opportunity:

- ▶ What is the financial condition of the prospect's company throughout the sales campaign? Will it be able to pay at the time the vendor is selected?

- ▶ What is the prospect's budget for investment in your product or service? Has the company allocated enough funds? What evidence do you have that the budget will remain intact? What other initiatives or contingencies may threaten the budget?

- ▶ What are the decision criteria, and their priorities, for each key decision maker, influencer, recommender, or buyer? Have these criteria changed? Who formulated them? (Your competitor? You've probably already lost.)

**See chapter
12 for more on
this subject.**

- ▶ Who are your competitors? What they are selling? Who are they selling it to? While you're calling on an accounting manager, is your competition in the CFO's office? If so, you may already have lost the deal.

- ▶ How are you, your company, your offering, and your proposed business contribution perceived by key recommenders, buyers, influencers, and decision makers? What about your competition?

- ▶ Do you have evidence that your prospective customers will actually make the purchase when they say they will? What happens to them, and to their business, if they don't? If your answer is "nothing," their decision could be postponed, perhaps indefinitely.

◀ We call this "slippage."

▶ What effort on your company's part will be required to sustain your efforts and win the deal? Are the resources available for this effort?

▶ What internal politics are influencing the evaluation? Who will make the final decision, and by what process? The competitor who best advances the decision makers' agendas will probably win the deal.

▶ How close a relationship can you expect to establish with the prospect? Will you be treated as simply a vendor on demand? Or is the client, like some of the Global 100, looking for a long-term strategic partner?

Winners have mastered the skill of objective, diligent qualification. Like pilots, they understand that you must be constantly scanning the instrument panel, because once you see trouble, it may be too late.

TACTIC: Get connected with the appropriate people in your company and dissect the last big purchase your company made. Go back over the questions above and determine how well qualified your company would have appeared to the winner and the losers of that deal. You'll gain real insight into the qualification process from a buyer's perspective, which will help you sell better.

Chapter 10

"No Matter What, I'll Never Give Up!"

STRATEGY #10. BECOME ADEPT AT PERFORMING TRIAGE

Now you have learned to perform objective, diligent qualification. The next step is to use the information from the qualification process to weigh one opportunity against another, so you can decide where to invest your time to get the greatest return.

Merriam-Webster Collegiate Dictionary

That's where triage comes in. One definition of "triage" is "the assigning of priority order to projects on the basis of where funds and resources can be best used or are most needed." This definition is what I mean when I use the word. However, the original meaning of triage is to the same point but more heart wrenching: it is the practice by medical personnel, when treating multiple casualties, of determining whether a person's injuries are (1) life-threatening but survivable if treated immediately, (2) fatal whether treated or not, or (3) not life threatening and therefore not requiring immediate attention. Triage is performed to determine how to allocate a limited supply of medical treatment to maximize survival.

Triage for sales opportunities can be similarly categorized. The ability to assess each situation objectively and act according to the facts will lead to a successful outcome — winning more business.

How do you apply triage to your sales opportunities? Like the emergency medical technician, the top sales professional understands that time and resources are the limiting factors. Here's how it works.

My guess is that right now you are pursuing three categories of deals:

1. Deals you cannot win.

2. Deals you cannot lose.

3. Deals you can win if you apply your best efforts.

Knowing how to divide your valuable time and effort among these categories can put you on the road to being a winning sales professional.

> *"One-half of knowing what you want is knowing what you must give up before you get it."*
>
> — SIDNEY HOWARD

LOST CAUSES

Some sales opportunities are not true opportunities. They are unqualified, not worth spending any time or resources on, for various reasons: no budget, no evaluation plan, no executive backing them. Others you will lose, if you have not already lost, to a competitor. If you know you've already lost an opportunity with two months to go in the evaluation, what should you do?

It depends on the situation. In general, however, you shouldn't withdraw completely. A skilled sales professional can gain competitive insight by staying in the game, while at the same time keeping a competitor distracted from other opportunities by forcing him to work harder on a deal he's probably already won.

Years ago I worked with a strong sales rep who knew how to derive maximum advantage from dead-end opportunities. She diligently monitored the progress of the evaluation. Even when she lost, which was not often, she stayed in the game until the final bell. In one case, she advised the prospect to demand a conference-room pilot demonstration using the winning competitor's system, and even provided the names of the competitor's key technical people. Very smart selling, for two reasons. First, she was tying up her competitor's most effective personnel in pursuit of business they had already won. Second, running a pilot was risky for the competitor because product deficiencies might be exposed before the deal was finalized. And if that happened, she was ready to jump back into the fray.

Be advised, however, that dogged persistence has its own risks. Monitoring a lost situation is one thing; it's a different matter entirely to keep believing "I can win this thing, if only. . . ." Give it up. You're better off diverting your resources to opportunities in the next two categories.

> A skilled sales professional can gain competitive insight by staying in the game, while at the same time keeping a competitor distracted from other opportunities by forcing him to work harder on a deal he's probably already won.

YOURS TO LOSE

There are deals you will most definitely win, if indeed you don't already have them locked up. Perhaps the key buyer, influencer, or decision maker has told you, in unambiguous terms, that you have been or will be selected. Your competition has been eliminated but is being strung along to reassure the purchasing VP or evaluation committee that the final decision is not entirely out of their hands.

When you find yourself in this situation, stay close to the people who swung the decision in your favor. Monitor the process, reinforce your position, validate their judgment — and above all, don't get complacent.

That said, if you're sure you've won, free up some of your time to pursue other opportunities that could go either way — like those in the next category. That's where you'll get the greatest return on your investment of time, resources, and attention.

YOURS TO WIN

The diligence and objectivity of your qualification process has led you to conclude that in many of your sales opportunities, although you haven't yet locked up the deal, you're still a strong contender. These are the ones that remind you of the true nature of competition. It's combat on two fronts, and the adversary with the best combination of business value and sales know-how takes the victory. These are the campaigns where a strong sales plan, well executed, will make the difference between winning and losing. And needless to say, these opportunities are where you should focus all the time and attention you can safely free up from the other two categories.

SORTING THEM OUT

Let's say you're pursuing twenty opportunities in all. You have to close one per quarter to exceed your quota by 25 percent, which is your personal minimum. How do you decide which opportunities to invest most of your time in and where to invest the least? It goes right back to objective, continuing, vigilant qualification — looking realistically at all your opportunities and categorizing them as (1) locked up or likely, (2) going or gone, or (3) possible.

Using the qualification criteria listed in chapter 9, rank your opportunities objectively. If you find this difficult, it's probably for one of three reasons:

▶ it's too early in the deal;

▶ you haven't asked the right people the right questions; or

▶ you're emotionally involved and can't be objective.

This last reason can be particularly insidious in undermining your qualification process. Triage must be performed unemotionally as well as objectively. Emotion is important in selling. You need to be passionate about helping your customer achieve success (and about your own as well); you need enthusiasm for your company and its offerings; you need rapport with the people you're selling to as well as your own team members. You certainly need a strong desire to win. But when it comes to qualification and triage, keep the emotion out.

> You certainly need a strong desire to win. But when it comes to qualification and triage, keep the emotion out.

MONEY IN YOUR POCKET

Why is triage so important in competitive selling? Because in the winning strategies I'm recommending in this book, you have to give more, not less, attention to each opportunity; to dig deeper and expand your knowledge of the customer, his market, and your competitor. You have to spend time building relationships with key people in the account.

See Strategy #15.

The time it takes to accomplish all this has to come from somewhere, right? Where it comes from is the time you save by not pursuing deals you can't win or that aren't worth winning, or by not spending inappropriate amounts of time in comfortable situations with people who have already indicated they'll buy from you.

TACTIC: Do you really believe a particular opportunity is qualified and worth pursuing? Give it the acid test. Ask yourself: "If I had to fund every penny of my salary, benefits, expenses, and other costs of acquiring this contract, in return for, say, reimbursement and a 30 to 40 percent commission, would I do it?" Makes your collar feel a bit tight, doesn't it? That's the bet your company is making. That's why it's your responsibility to be logical, objective, diligent, and unemotional in pursuing the right deals.

Time is money, right? The time you've freed up, the time that you've turned to productive purposes — that's money in your pocket.

Chapter 11

"Correct Me If I'm Wrong, But . . ."

▶ STRATEGY #11. SCRUTINIZE YOUR PROSPECT

In the information age, information is not only an asset, it's an essential tool. It is your number-one lever, the one you use to gain and maintain differentiation and credibility — to transform yourself into your client's trusted advisor, immune from competition.

There's a lot of information out there. What sources and types do you need most? In this chapter I will describe

109
△

the kinds of information you should concentrate on obtaining, and where you can look for it. When you follow these guidelines, the information you gather on each client will become the situation assessment component of your plan for achieving the sale. In acquiring this information, you will expand your network into new areas both inside and outside your target company. The growth of your network will increase your selling success, both short term and long term.

As you read through this chapter, you'll begin to realize how much you didn't know about your prospects in deals you have lost. In hindsight, you may recognize that your competitor knew more about the prospect than you — and used that knowledge to win the deal.

When you're selling a strategic solution, your chances of success are small unless you tie your product or service in specific, measurable financial terms to your prospect's goals and objectives. You simply cannot construct a plausible ROI model projecting specific improvements unless you truly understand the prospect's business.

To do this, you need three kinds of information:

1. General and specific information about the prospect's industry

2. General and specific information about the prospect company

3. Crucial advance information about the prospect's executives (things you need to know before you call on them)

Gathering and analyzing this information takes time. However, it's easier to get started if you remember these points:

▶ Your skill at triage will free up more time to gather crucial information on qualified prospects.

▶ Scrutinizing prospects gets easier with practice. You learn what information to focus on and where to find it, and you get positive feedback from prospects when you use the information effectively. You get information in return for information.

▶ Knowing your prospect gives you confidence. When you can walk into an executive's office prepared to talk knowledgeably with her about her company, her industry, and her world, your competence shines through.

TACTIC: For a deeper understanding of the issues, spend some time applying each question below to your industry, your company, and your executive management team. You may be shocked to see what you don't know. Be sure to answer every question before you go on to the next one. Don't cheat. This exercise will make you money!

INDUSTRY INFORMATION

Here's what you need to know or find out about the industry you're selling to.

▶ What industry history must you know in order to be credible to your prospect's executives? For example, few pharmaceutical industry executives would consider you a potential business partner unless you understood the ins and outs of the stringent FDA regulations they must comply with.

▶ What trends affect the near and distant future of your prospect's industry? For example, what will be the ultimate impact of the Internet on your customers who happen to be book publishers or paper companies?

"The secret of success is to know something nobody else knows."

— ARISTOTLE ONASSIS

▶ Who's the winner in that marketplace — your prospect, or the prospect's biggest competitor? Is market leadership up for grabs?

▶ How did the market leaders get to be the leaders? What was their strategy? Is it different from your prospect's strategy? What strategies are the leaders employing to stay in front?

TACTIC: When performing research on your prospect, ask yourself, "How can my product or service help this company become the leader?" That's probably a favorite topic of your prospect's executives.

▶ Who are the market losers? How did they wind up in that position? Were they ever on top? How long did it take them to get from where they were to where they are? Could your company have done anything to prevent it? What actions are they now taking to recover? Can your offering help?

▶ How much do you know about the best practices of your industry? Are you selling customer service improvement programs to a chain of department stores? If you are, you'd better understand how that industry measures Nordstrom's success.

▶ Which analysts watch the industry? There are securities analysts, such as those who work for Merrill Lynch or Dain Bosworth, and there are industry analysts, like the Gartner Group. Once you know who these analysts are, find out what they are saying about your industry: Is it healthy? Growing? Declining? Don't forget about the industry pundits, luminaries, and visionaries. Who are they? What are they saying? Who in your prospect's company listens to them? Ask your company's marketing and investor relations people who those leaders are.

See chapter 6. ▶

▶ Are you reading your prospect's industry trade journals as if you were a player? If not, you'll never be one.

▶ Are you spending enough time attending and contributing to trade association meetings and events?

I know that gathering this information requires a big investment, but don't limit your earning potential by short-changing your credibility, value, and staying power in front of the executives you will be calling on.

Where do you get the time? Read about triage in chapter 10.

COMPANY INFORMATION

Let's have a look at what you need to know about the company you are selling to. Of course, some of the information you gather may make you realize you don't want to pursue business with that company. But that's good news, too. It lets you free up time for more qualified prospects.

Just as you did with its industry, start with the company's history.

▶ You should know why, when, and how the company was founded. Who founded it? What was the founder's background and vision? What are the company's major victories and defeats? Are there subjects you should not broach? On the other hand, perhaps they deserve congratulations for a major victory that you should know about, such as being awarded a patent or achieving their own big sales win.

▶ What is the company's position now compared with 5, 15, or 25 years ago? Five, 15, or 25 months ago? Whether it is better or worse, you should know the reason. They may be skyrocketing, but is it because they've successfully executed their plan? Or is it because their major competitor is focusing on another market?

▶ Is your prospect involved in a joint venture or other alliance? If so, your best customer may be a current or future business partner of that company — a fact that could be of great help in your planning.

This process of gathering information is not going to be helpful if you wait until the day before you call on a senior

△

executive for the first time. Begin scrutinizing your prospect at least five days ahead of time. That will give you time to locate sources and to dig up, analyze, internalize, and communicate to your sales team everything you need to make yourself an expert.

Here are some other valuable things to find out:

▶ Does your prospect have a mission statement or a corporate value statement? How does it compare with yours? Will doing business with your company conflict with, advance, or support your prospect's mission or values?

▶ What are the specifics of your prospect's corporate culture? Some companies require employees to respond to voice mail messages within four business hours. At others, the parking lots are empty at 8:58 in the morning and again at 5:02 in the afternoon. An engineer-turned-sales-manager I know walks through a prospect's parking lot before a first meeting, counting reserved spots, tabulating car models and conditions, noting bumper stickers and other cultural clues.

▶ How often does your prospect file lawsuits? Does the company like to sue? It's a good idea to know this going in.

▶ Are there other business or nonbusiness issues that could help you understand the company better? Did they place first in the local Corporate Challenge 10K race? Are they listed among the top ten best places to work? Fifteen years ago I was immersed in a selling cycle with a major chemical company. Since I was vigilantly tracking them in the news (there was no Internet then) I caught the story: they were under investigation for allegedly dumping toxic waste thirty years before. As you can well imagine, investing in my solution quickly became the last thing on their minds.

▶ Who's on the management team? Start with names and titles. Is there much turnover? When changes are made, where do the senior executives come from — sales and marketing, or engineering? The answer will tell you a lot about how the company's focus will shift. If top positions are filled from outside, are the new recruits coming mostly from one company? Your prospect may begin operating more like that company.

▶ Who sits on the board of directors? Mostly insiders? What other boards do these people sit on? These are general questions about the executive team; we'll get more specific later.

▶ What are your prospect's products or services? You need to be able to speak knowledgeably and comfortably, in the company's terms, about everything from new product introductions to lead times for custom orders. You should also understand which markets they serve. Which products or services have the biggest profit margins? Which have the smallest?

▶ What does your prospect count on to win — quality, price, innovation, name recognition, customer service? Does the company compete ethically, or does it do "whatever it takes to win"?

▶ Who are your prospect's major competitors? In my experience, knowing the names and products of your prospect's competitors counts for a lot with executives. Know how competitors are doing financially, what they do to win, where they are strong. Have any of them announced plans to expand into new markets? If you can hypothesize intelligently about the impact of a competitor's plans, you'll become almost indispensable to your prospect.

Learn as much as you can about your prospect's relationships with suppliers. This can tell you a lot about not only the impending evaluation process but also how you will work with the company if you win the evaluation. For example, it's very hard to sell long-term business value to a company whose raw materials and supplies are commodities. Their mindset is to get whatever they need from whoever can sell it to them at today's lowest price. It's important to know this early in the sales cycle, because your product or service is likely to be considered a commodity as well.

Speaking of suppliers, do you know who is now supplying your prospect with what you're selling? It's important to know why your prospect wants to change vendors. Ask your sources inside the account what the current supplier is doing or is expected to do to prevent you from taking over its customer.

Watch how your prospects treat their customers; it's a fair indication of how they expect to be treated by you. What does the company consider important for its customers? Is it the best products? Timely delivery? Superior relationships? Technical support? Does it use customer focus groups? Does it take pride in its research and development team? You can often go to the head of the pack if you know the answers early on and plan your sales activities accordingly.

What about the organization? What does your prospect's organization chart look like? How does the current chart compare with the one from last year, the year before, and the year before that? Spotting organizational trends can help

---

TACTIC: Notice how the sequential satellite photos and radar images you see on TV weathercasts enable you to predict the weather by extrapolating from past movements of clouds and rain. You can often use recent organization charts the same way. Ask your prospect for charts going back a few years. If your contacts can't (or won't) provide them, try to reconstruct them on your own. It will be worth your time and effort.

---

you anticipate changes and see more clearly who you should be talking to. For instance, does the corporation assign future general managers to overseas facilities to give them international experience?

Read your prospect's annual reports or other financial statements for the past few years. Look for performance trends; see if you can tell by extrapolation where your prospect is headed. If you've developed your business skills and know-how to become a better sales professional, you should feel right at home reading, understanding, and drawing conclusions from standard company financial reports. If not, you need a crash course. Enroll in classes, read books, get someone to help you learn this essential skill. Your prospect's website and www.freeedgar.com are good sources for historical financial statements.

See Strategy #5 for more information about this important subject.

Learn how your prospects measure themselves. Do they look at revenue, profit growth, market share growth, or some other parameter? (Companies in financial trouble will be tracking expense reduction.) If your business solution can help the prospect in one or more of these areas, discover your prospect's exact targets and the potential benefit you can deliver.

Because businesses differ in the ways they cost-justify investments and expenses, you need to find out how your proposal will eventually be considered. What areas is the company targeting for improvement in the next six, twelve, or thirty-six months? Knowing this will give you the basis for a solid cost/benefits analysis later on, when you propose your solution.

If you expect to get paid when you finally get the target company's business, you'd best know their payment history with vendors. To find out, get a report from Dun & Bradstreet.

If I were a company executive and you were a salesperson calling to represent a prospective vendor, I would probably

---

TACTIC: If your prospect is a public company, it is probably tracked by securities analysts. To gain access to an analyst's reports, it may be worth your while to open an account with the brokerage firm the analyst represents. These reports often contain information about your prospect's competitors and industry as well. Most of them are very informative and reasonably accurate, even if their predictions about the company's stock performance are at times dubious. If the prospect is privately held, your scrutiny of its financials will present more of a challenge. The best tactic is to build a network of sources within the company, starting with a sales rep, as suggested in chapter 1.

---

be polite but skeptical. But if you talked to me about my business in financial terms — comparing and contrasting me with my competitors, referring to specific customers and suppliers, analyzing and projecting trends related to our market share in the past, present, and future — I would consider you a sales professional of the highest caliber, a fellow businessperson, and I'd put your company at the top of my list of potential business partners. I'm sure you'd agree that the time you invested in learning about my company was well worth it.

EXECUTIVE INFORMATION

When you're selling to a large organization with a complex reporting structure, the volume of information you need to know about its executives can be staggering. The most effective method of learning it is to ask questions — a lot of questions — of just about anyone you meet in that account. People will often give you their opinions, insights, organization charts, executive bios from press kits, and all sorts of other information just for the asking.

A lot of information about high-profile companies can be found on the Internet. Press releases, company "about" web pages, and financial statements are good sources for background information on the executives you'll be meeting with next week. Keep in mind, however, that this information is only part of the picture. There's politics involved as well, and understanding it often requires a steady, coordinated effort by the whole sales team.

> The most effective method of learning about your prospect's executives is to ask lots of questions of just about anyone you meet in that account.

Politics aside, here are some of the kinds of preliminary information you'll need on your prospect's key executives. There are two main sources of information about the executives within your prospect's company. The first of these is whatever has been published. This can be printed material, but more and more information, both original and historical, is being published on the Internet. Once you get to the "about" page on your prospect's website, click on the "management" link. Other sources, such as articles and press releases, can be located using a search engine. Try using the company name, product names, and executives' names as key words. This will often produce "hits" with real value, such as a biography from a speech an executive gave at an industry conference.

The other main source of information is simply other people. As you build a network of lower-level sources in your prospect's company, ask lots of questions about top execs and decision makers. You'll begin to get a clearer picture of your key executive, the one you will call. Find out what you can from other suppliers, customers, and even competitors who know this person.

That, in a nutshell, is how you find information on key executives. Here is what you need to know about them:

▶ Where they live. Do any of them live in the same town or neighborhood as your CEO? Think of the possibilities.

▶ Their approximate ages.

▶ How long they've been with the company.

▶ What positions they've held in the company. Have they moved from one functional area to another or advanced within a single division?

▶ Where did they work before joining this company? What responsibilities did they have there? Why did they leave? Was your product or your competitor's product used at the former company?

▶ How did they get to their current company? Did someone personally recruit them? If so, who, when, and why?

▶ What experience have they had with projects or investments similar to what you will probably be proposing? Have they been involved in making the decisions? What was their decision-making process?

▶ What events, decisions, or actions caused them to rise in this organization or a prior one? This information can be very useful; it may reveal ways you and the business value you bring can help them advance further.

▶ What events, decisions, or actions may have temporarily limited their careers or influence? This would definitely be a subject to stay away from, at least on the first call.

▶ What civic, professional, or trade organizations are they involved in?

▶ Where did they go to school?

▶ Were they in the military?

▶ What are their hobbies? Golf? Biking? Skiing? I can't overstate how helpful this can be. Recently I was able to form relationships with a few very senior business people because of our shared interest in owning and piloting private aircraft.

A number of years ago, when I was selling enterprise application software, I was scrutinizing the evaluation team in an account I was pursuing. I learned from a coach I had developed in the account that a key influencer had played the trumpet professionally, in a past life, as had I. That discovery rewarded me in three ways. The first was the fun I had planning how I would let the influencer know. The second reward came while listening to jazz trumpeter Freddie Hubbard's records at his house on a Sunday afternoon as he helped me plan how to win his company's business. The third, and best, was bringing in my company's largest-ever deal a month earlier than I had predicted.

Here are some examples of the type of information that will put you way out in front of your competition, if you know how to get it and how to use it:

▶ What does that executive already know about you, and what has she already decided about your products or services, your company, your reputation? It's better to know you're up against a misconception or other negative judgment going in than to mistakenly assume that she is positive or even neutral about you.

▶ How does the executive make decisions? Does she go with her gut or agonize endlessly over details? Does she rely on a trusted advisor? If so, allocate some time to scrutinize the advisor as well.

▶ What are the executive's personal and professional needs and interests? To give her an emotional incentive to buy from you, you'll need to know a lot more about her than her name and title. Does she have an infirm relative, which would make her reluctant to travel? Is she up for a promotion she's been working for years to get? Would investing in your business solution help or hinder her career goals? Would it entail too much or too little risk? These are things you need to know if you hope to link your needs to hers.

If you are looking for differentiation and willing to take the time to do what I recommend to execute this strategy, any manager or executive will be extremely impressed by what you know about her industry, her company, and the people she works with. You will have differentiated yourself!

WHEN TO SCRUTINIZE

Not every sales campaign, of course, requires you to scrutinize all aspects of an opportunity. You'll find that a comprehensive dossier is most useful for high-value, highly competitive deals. The time you spend scrutinizing each opportunity should be directly proportional to its financial or strategic importance.

> The time you spend scrutinizing each opportunity should be directly proportional to its financial or strategic importance.

You will use the information you gather in many ways while planning and executing your sales strategy. It will help you understand what your prospects are really buying, how they make decisions, who is in a position of influence, who initially favors you and who doesn't, how they will negotiate, whether they are true to their word, whether you have a chance to win the deal, and ultimately, how you will be able to win it.

Now that you understand the kind of information needed for the successful pursuit of an account, the question arises once more: "Where will I find the time to gather all this information?" My answer, as before: By reallocating time from wasteful sales activities. That's where the skill of tri-age applies.

See Strategy #10. ▶

Where Does It Hurt?

STRATEGY #12. KNOW WHAT YOUR CUSTOMER IS BUYING BEFORE YOU BEGIN SELLING

It's a mistake that's made every day. Following up on a sales lead, the sales rep finds someone in the prospect's organization who's willing to listen. Then it's off to the races — the rep launches into his spiel, telling his contact everything he never wanted to know about his product or service. The rep thinks he's differentiating his offering — and he is, in a way.

123
△

What he doesn't understand is that he's jumping the gun. He's positioning his product or service before he knows exactly what the prospect wants or needs. And once the offering is positioned in the prospect's mind, it's hard to reposition it.

Your prospect may well understand what you are selling or you wouldn't be there in the first place. But your job as a sales professional is to position your product or service against the continually changing decision criteria of the customer — *after* you know what they are.

Sales winners have the ability to create and maintain a dynamic balance in positioning their offerings. They provide enough information to keep the prospect interested, but not so much that they can't reposition as the prospect's unstated requirements come to light.

A rule of thumb: Before you irrevocably position your offering, you should have a pretty good idea of how it will be received. Will the prospects be excited, enticed? Will your positioning meet their expectations, raise a concern, change their minds for or against you? Will it educate them, or will it threaten them?

ASSUME NOTHING

When RFPs, RFIs, or other formal documents are presented, you will often be left with an impression of what the prospects are looking for. However, without a clear explanation of their situation and what they believe to be the solution, you can't assume anything.

As an everyday example, think about the popularity of the ubiquitous sports utility vehicle. Why do people buy these vehicles? Lots of reasons: to carry their children, their

> *"If you only have a hammer, you tend to see every problem as a nail."*
>
> — ABRAHAM MASLOW

children's friends, skis, bikes, fishing poles, dogs large and small, lots of packages; to navigate through snow, mud, and bad weather; to drive over the mountains, through the woods, across the desert, and along the beach; to protect themselves from other drivers; to intimidate other drivers. . . .

In most cases, the buyer envisions how she will be using the vehicle long before she arrives at the automobile dealership. And here's what often happens: The salesperson sees her eyeing the SUV and immediately starts pitching how great it is for carrying her kids to the soccer match, how the hubby will love it, and so forth. But it turns out that the prospect is single and happens to be an emergency-room physician who needs to get to the hospital no matter what the weather. The salesperson has already lost credibility with that potential buyer. Had the salesperson simply asked the prospect some pointed questions about her needs, he might have started a positive dialogue. As a buyer, haven't you had this experience a few times?

Before a company or a department begins to evaluate a potential investment in a product or service, usually someone high up in the company has already envisioned most of the benefits, both hard and soft, he expects the company to derive.

We talked about the hard benefits earlier. Remember the timeless truth about sales? That's right: it all comes down to money. Your product or service, if purchased, is expected to bring the company greater profitability. Period.

The soft benefits are a different story. These are the benefits your prospects have not envisioned — the additional value your offering will bring to the company. Soft benefits can be what truly differentiate your offering from your competitor's. When prospects seem inclined to view your product or service as a commodity, you can often swing the evaluation in your favor by bringing unforeseen soft benefits to their attention.

This is why you must understand your prospects' vision of the solution before you start telling them what color it will be or how much horsepower it will have or how many

125

terabytes of storage it will contain or how it will make their job better and their children rich.

We're not talking about anything terribly complex here. It's a lot like what you learned in Sales 101: "Mr. Prospect, if you could design the perfect whatchamacallit, what would it look like?" The difference today is what we talked about at the beginning of this book — commoditization, caused by the proliferation of what the buyer sees as similar products and the resulting inclination to buy on price alone.

DON'T PRE-PRESCRIBE

The temptation to immediately position your offering is strong. Trying to grab mindshare, you are driven to pre-prescribe — to get out in front of your prospects, tell them how you're different, what you've done for other companies like theirs, what you can do for them. But telling them what you believe they need before you understand what *they* believe they need just makes you more of a commodity. Why? Because you're basing your position on a known set of requirements for a broad range of companies. It's the equivalent of "Take an aspirin and call me in the morning."

What I am recommending instead is today's version of "Mr. Prospect, if you could have the perfect whatchamacallit. . . ?" By avoiding pre-prescribing, you're more likely to gain access to organizational leaders with whom you can discover new issues and develop unique approaches. As any successful consultant will tell you, that's where the big bucks are. "Seek first to understand, then be understood," wrote Stephen Covey in *7 Habits of Highly Effective People.* That's excellent advice.

Once you've proven you're an industry expert, researched your prospect, learned all you can about the decision makers, and understood the published decision criteria, you're in position to differentiate yourself from your competition. You can say, "Mr. Prospect, based on our discussions of your business plan, my experience in your industry, and my understanding of what you expect to accomplish by investing in a whatchamacallit, I think you're in for a surprise. My offering can bring you benefits far beyond what you expect, some of which probably haven't occurred to you."

"TELL ME MORE"

With that statement, or its real-life equivalent, you've probably gained enough differentiation and credibility to get that executive on your side. And if his response is at all positive — "Tell me more" — you can begin to take control of the decision criteria. Once you've got the football, you can run over the competition.

"Tell me more" is your first goal. When they hear that, winners start the next scoring drive by asking the executive to set you up with key members of his management team. "Here's what we have to do," they say. "I'll need about forty-five minutes each with Paul Browne, Nancy Chin, Raul Gomez, and Ed Rosenfeld over the next week to see what my solution might contribute to their departments. I'll gather

---

TACTIC: Here's one to take you out of your comfort zone. During your next sales call, early in the prospect's buying process, offer nothing but questions. Make them relevant, insightful, and thought-provoking, but — unless you are specifically asked to respond to a question yourself — only ask questions. You'll find this exercise will force you to think more diagnostically. And if you haven't read Stephen Covey's *7 Habits of Highly Effective People* in the last eighteen months, read it again.

---

and analyze the data, and I'll report back to you, let's say, a week from today. If I see at any point that there's no good reason to go on with this process, I'll cancel our meeting and take no more of your time. But I believe the benefits will be substantial."

Now, here's where you go for your second, and most important, goal. You say, "If you're prepared to tell those four executives what I'm proposing, I can start my discovery tomorrow morning."

If the exec says no, either (1) he's not buying, (2) he is buying, but not from you, or (3) he's a commodity buyer who will look for the cheapest solution, not the highest value.

If he says yes, you've earned yourself not only a return visit but his backing to work with key managers on a bigger business solution to a broader need.

And that's how the winners do it.

Part

Getting into the Game

Having invested considerable time in this book, you should be ready, perhaps eager, to apply at least some of these strategies toward your goal of outselling your competition and winning the big sale.

Now it's time to talk about some of the tools you will need in order to fully implement these strategies. By the end of this part of *How Winners Sell:*

▶ You will be able to write a simple yet highly effective sales plan and understand that the benefits of that plan far outweigh any inconvenience or investment of time involved.

▶ You'll be able to create a clear, concise, compelling executive presentation.

▶ You'll understand how, and with which people in your accounts, to build relationships.

Plan to Win the Sale

W hen I make a presentation to a group of salespeople, I often ask, "How many of you create a formal written plan, however simple, for each important opportunity you are pursuing?" In these unscientific surveys, fewer than 5 percent of my audience raise their hands.

I can only surmise that, if you're the average salesperson, you don't have a sales plan. Perhaps you don't think you need one. "Too much trouble," you say. "Eats into my selling time. Besides, what good is a plan when you can't possibly tell in advance what's going to happen?"

I understand your reluctance to plan, but I don't buy your reasoning. Neither do the million-dollar earners.

What if other professionals thought this way?

▶ The airline pilot says, "No, I haven't filed a flight plan, but I expect the weather will be good all the way to Chicago, and if it isn't, I'll fake it."

▶ The builder says, "Just start nailing some of those boards together and we'll decide later whether it's one story or two."

▶ The surgeon says, "Aw, what the heck, let's start cutting and see what happens."

Anyone whose livelihood depends on the quality and reliability of his work makes a fundamental mistake when he fails to plan. When you don't know what's going to happen, it's especially important to plan for contingencies. You may not know at the start of a trip whether it will rain or shine, whether the road is good or bad, whether the lodging is cheap or expensive — so you bring your umbrella, a spare tire, and your credit cards. That's simple planning.

As you probably know, an airline pilot must file a flight plan with the Federal Aviation Administration detailing exact route, time en route, fuel reserves, type of navigation equipment used, and souls on board. The builder must follow a

> *"Virtually all of my questions at the trial, and most of my tactics and techniques, are aimed at enabling me to make arguments I've already determined I want to make. In fact, before the first witness at a trial has even been called, I've usually prepared my summation to the jury."*
>
> — VINCENT BUGLIOSI

blueprint, schedule deliveries of building materials, and bring in skilled workers and subcontractors at the right times. The surgeon must outline in detail the operation to be performed, equipment and personnel needed, sequence of procedures, condition and idiosyncrasies of the patient, and postoperative care required. In each of these examples, you can see that planning not only maps out the best route to a successful outcome, it also enables everyone involved to communicate and coordinate team activities.

Following a planning process is a sort of rehearsal or walk-through: What do you do first? What comes next? If you're familiar with the steps, you'll find your plan easier to follow when it's for real. Planning is also a kind of advance troubleshooting: What do you do if this happens? How do you respond if that part of the plan fizzles? How do you know if you're on track toward your objective? Thus, even if your original plan doesn't work as expected, the process of planning is essential to achieving and maintaining sales success. It forces you to anticipate eventualities and compels you to action.

THE SALES PLANNING PROCESS

The simplest and most effective sales planning template is one that's commonly used in complex, large-account selling. It's the same four-part model I used in planning this book: assessing the situation, setting your objective, devising your strategy for achieving that objective, and choosing the tactics you will use to implement your strategy.

When building a sales plan using this model, the part that's most often neglected is the first step. This is a big mistake; you have to know where you're starting from in order to decide where you can reasonably end up. For a

> *"It's not the plan that is important, it's the planning."*
>
> — DR. GRAEME EDWARDS

△

solid, workable plan, you must start by assessing the situation. What is your prospect's business need, and what is the sales environment?

Once you've compiled a comprehensive review of your sales opportunity, you can move on to the next step — deciding on your sales objective. With your objective as the target, you can select and refine your strategy for reaching that objective. Then, to execute that strategy, you choose the most appropriate tactics.

The biggest challenge I run into when first working with a sales team is to help them avoid jumping straight to tactics. We've just started to talk about key factors in the prospect's industry when the sales rep says, "Let's call Ms. Newman and tell her about our new variable-speed, dynamic-tilt garfiplatzer. I'm sure she'll love it." Or we're busy deciphering the subtleties of an organization chart that the rep finally got his hands on after five calls to his contact in the account, and a business consultant says, "Wait. I know Bill Hines. He and I played football together at Whatever U. I'll call him and set up a demonstration."

Think of the four components of your sales plan as building blocks. When one is solidly in place, the next is laid atop it:

4	Tactics
3	Strategy
2	Objective
1	Situation Assessment

I'm sure these examples of the "ready, fire, aim" syndrome must sound familiar. Sometimes, during a lively meeting, I even catch myself trying to jump the gun. Anything that results in getting more information about the prospect and completing the situation assessment is allowable; however, brainstorming at this stage should not extend to selling tactics.

THE SITUATION ASSESSMENT

Let's say you've been scrutinizing your prospect. You've dug deep into your prospect's business and have gathered most of the material you need for your business summary: financial statements, press releases, articles, company information, interview notes, organization charts, analysts' reports. You've also learned who's competing, how they compete, and how your prospect views you versus your competition. Not least in importance, you've gained information that will help you qualify the prospect.

See Strategy #11.

So — now that you've gathered the information, the work is done, right?

Wrong. Now you have to write it down.

Why? Two reasons: First, you don't analyze your prospect's business just to make yourself look smart; you use it to coordinate your entire sales effort. You have to get the information to other members of your sales team, and to your executives when they join your campaign.

Second, you're a busy sales rep, managing several opportunities at once, and you're juggling a flood of information. If you don't keep detailed, well-organized written notes or enter all crucial information into your computer, you will invariably forget vital details or, worse, remember them wrong or get your prospects mixed up. Details are not trivial. Command of detail gives you credibility and differentiation with your prospect's executives; it can spell the difference between failure and success.

Chapter 16 will provide more detail on details.

Sales reps have griped at me for years because I insist the information must be recorded, whether electronically or in writing. Takes too much time, they say. This is wrong. If you've got your priorities straight, most of the time you invest in reviewing your prospect's business will be the time required simply to hunt down the information. Typing it into your computer or collating hard copies into folders for your team will be a breeze, relatively speaking. (Leading customer relationship management applications make this task easier and faster.) One of the most effective sales professionals I know spends 85 percent of her prospect assessment time collecting information, only 15 percent recording and distributing it.

> Most of the time you invest in reviewing your prospect's business will be the time required simply to hunt down the information.

△

Not important, you say? Either you're not serious about winning the deal, or you simply don't realize how useful this information can be when written down.

Aaron, a sales professional I work with in Southern California, knows the value of having it in writing. For each key prospect, he puts together a three-ring loose-leaf binder of information on the opportunity, the proposed business solution, and the competition. In a meeting one day with a prospect, the company's CFO asked, "What's that?"

"It's information I've collected about your company and this business opportunity."

"Could I see it?"

"Sure," said Aaron. Smiling, he handed it over.

The section on competition included press releases from other vendors vying for the business. Aaron had highlighted certain passages and, clearly and legibly, had written comments in the margins that raised questions about the integrity and capability of his competitors. The CFO read quietly for many minutes, paying particular attention to those comments. He took some notes. Aaron ended up winning the sale.

> A situation assessment is a dynamic, ever-changing compilation. It is never "finished."

Keep in mind that a situation assessment is a dynamic, ever-changing compilation. It is never "finished." Over the three, nine, or twenty-four months of your selling effort, market conditions will change, affecting not only your sales campaign but your prospect's business condition. When do you know enough? How do you know when you're ready to go to the next step? When you can confidently envision exactly what you will sell, when, and at what price, in this unique situation.

THE OBJECTIVE

Too many sales reps just plod through customer buying cycles, following the prospect's plan — if not the competitor's — hoping perhaps to win when someone else stumbles. The thought of taking control of what's happening doesn't occur to them. They have no objective, nothing to aim for, no clear mission, and therefore, ultimately, no way to achieve it.

Winners know that when scrutinizing their prospect they can develop a keen understanding of what the company will buy, when they will buy it, how much they will invest in it, and — most important for the prospect — what buying it will do for the bottom line. Winners also know that by putting all this information on record for their sales teams and executives, they begin to take control of the situation by formulating a firm, achievable sales objective.

Why do we use the term "objective" here rather than "goal"? According to the Educational Technology Department at San Diego State University:

▶ Goals are broad; objectives are narrow.

▶ Goals are general intentions; objectives are precise.

▶ Goals are intangible; objectives are tangible.

▶ Goals are abstract; objectives are concrete.

▶ Goals can't be validated as is; objectives can be validated.

In terms of a sales campaign, your objective includes precisely what you intend to sell to the prospect, for how much, and by when. If you fail to define any part of this objective, you can't formulate an effective strategy, and you'll find it hard to achieve the sale under favorable terms.

And, please, aim for a financially lofty objective. Think big! It benefits your career as well as your wallet to justify why a prospect should pay full price.

See chapter 3 on retooling for selling BIG.

STRATEGY

The heart of your sales plan is your strategy. Just as the twenty-one strategies that outline this book are crucial in raising your sales capabilities to a new level, your sales strategy is what you count on to win the sale.

In sales, your strategy is based on three things:

1. the key values or benefits your offering has for meeting your prospect's business needs and requirements (as you know them from your situation assessment);

2. your prospect's ability and willingness to buy (which you have determined through vigilant qualification); and

3. your prospect's perception of you and your competitors.

Here are some of the many values, benefits, and conditions on which winners I've worked with have based their sales strategies:

▶ The best product or service for the prospect's requirements, as specified in their buying criteria

▶ The value you can provide above and beyond your standard offering, such as your ability to meet unstated requirements or unrecognized needs or to provide effective resources

▶ Current and future relationships with key people in your prospect's organization

Donald G. Krause, *The Art of War for Executives*, p. 34 (Perigee Books)

On the subject of strategy, Sun Tzu, the ancient general and philosopher, said, "A great general [or sales professional] establishes his position where he cannot be defeated. He misses no opportunity to exploit the weaknesses of his enemy. A winning general creates the conditions of victory before beginning the war. A losing general begins the war without knowing how to win it."

▶ The sales strategies, schemes, and tactics your competitors have traditionally employed (avoiding their strengths, highlighting their weaknesses)

▶ Your personal integrity — or your competitor's lack of integrity

▶ The surety associated with your offering or company

▶ Your company's unique ability to give your prospect competitive advantage in his marketplace

Be clear on your strategy, but learn to expect the unexpected. Mergers, acquisitions, reassignment of key personnel, changes in strategic direction, new competitors, as well as regional, national, global, or industry-wide economic trends — these things happen, more often than ever in today's business world. Your assessment of the prospect's situation must be kept current, and any change should cause you immediately to reconsider your sales plan, to adapt even the cleverest strategy.

GE's former CEO Jack Welch knows the shortcomings of strategic planning in business. He quotes a letter written by a Bendix planning manager to *FORTUNE* magazine:

> Detailed planning necessarily failed, due to the inevitable frictions encountered: chance events, imperfections in execution, and the independent will of the opposition. . . . Any cookbook approach is powerless to cope with independent will, or with the unfolding situations of the real world.

◀ *Jack Welch, Jack: Straight from the Gut,* p. 448.

The same is true for sales professionals. Every day in the field brings changes, new challenges, that we must adapt to. Fortunately for us, a sales plan is only a microcosm of the kind of massive strategic business planning that Welch talks about. No one could have foreseen the terrible events of September 11, 2001, and their impact on the economy, our businesses, and our lives; but when major changes occur in the business climate, a sales strategy is easier and faster to change than a corporate business plan.

△

See chapter 5. ▶

Knowledge is the key. Your ability to anticipate how such events affect sales is directly related to your knowledge of each account, your relationships within it, and a keen understanding of the competition, your target market, and the way the business world works. In other words, you need to think like a businessperson, not just a salesperson. When you do, you tune in to the signs and signals that changes are coming. And by selling business value, rather than just the products or services that deliver it, you position yourself with key people in your accounts who can provide the business information you need.

So how, you ask, can anybody plan strategy without knowing what changes lie ahead? Isn't it an exercise in futility to plan a detailed strategy, when everyone knows things will change but no one knows what the changes will be?

Keep in mind two words: "reasonable" and "flexible." Your strategy should be reasonably detailed, down to the level where you are comfortable improvising the finer points in the field. And it should be flexible — readily adaptable when you have to change direction unexpectedly.

Be flexible; don't overplan. But above all, plan.

TACTICS

Now, you say to yourself: "I have done a comprehensive assessment of the opportunity. I have committed to a sales objective. I've decided on a strategy I'm going to pursue to win. What's next?" What's next is what you're going to use to implement your strategy — the sales execution, or tactics.

Tactical planning is simple if you have the first three components of your sales plan in place. Once you know what resources and advantages you're going to count on to achieve your win — that is, your strategy — tactics are simply the events, meetings, phone calls, presentations, demonstrations, proposal submissions, contracts, RFPs, referral calls, visits, and — most important — informal discussions that you will need to conduct to reach your objective.

I'll provide more detail in chapter 16. ▶

I've found a simple spreadsheet to be a good tool for tactical planning:

Account Name	Date	Event	Owner	Resources Required	Objective	Result
ABC Corp	6/10	Initial Exec Presentation with CEO and CFO	Stein	Fran Jones, our CFO	Get buy-in for discovery process	
XYZ, Inc	6/11	Get our contract to their legal department	Stein	Jim Kownsell, our atty	Get negotiations started	
123 Co	6/11	Dinner with VP Sales	Stein	None	Relationship building, find out more about informal decision process	

I like this format because in a single document I can keep track of everything I have to do in several accounts. I can sort the spreadsheet by account, date (as shown here), or owner, as well as by resource required (so I can be sure the help I require is there when I need it). You may prefer to keep track of plans and activities another way, using sales automation or contact management software. That's fine, as long as you're tracking every part of your plan. But if you're looking at this and thinking, "That's too much work. I can do just fine keeping this in my head," let me remind you of how important even the smallest details can be. Tactics are, after all, where the rubber meets the road when you're carrying out your sales plan.

I'll talk a lot more about detail in chapter 16, and I'll give you the foundation for a valuable checklist for all your selling tactics.

Earlier, we posed a common objection: "What good is a plan when you can't possibly tell in advance what's going to happen?" Now you have the answer: What's going to happen is what you plan to happen, so long as your plans are flexible enough to adapt to a changing sales environment.

If you need more encouragement to jump out of your comfort zone and do some formal sales planning, consider this: it gets easier each time you do it. It really does. After you've planned and won three or four sales campaigns this way, you'll begin to think habitually in sales planning terms:

▶   Whenever you scan a newspaper, a magazine, or a content-rich website, your attention will automatically be drawn to news about your prospects, your competitors, your industry. You will begin to capture account information that will help you pursue and win sales opportunities.

▶   You will begin to recognize how companies outside your industry position themselves, what strategies they employ, and what they count on to win (based on messages they deliver through advertising, press releases, and articles). How does McDonald's battle Burger King? What strategy does Avis use against Hertz?

▶   You will begin to ask your prospects new questions and watch closely their every move. Not only will they evaluate you, but you will probe *them*, you will validate *them*, you will qualify *them*.

▶   You will begin to pursue your sales objectives like a heat-seeking missile.

TACTIC: If you have never done it before, write down or electronically record your sales plan, starting now.

Chapter  14

►"Do I Have That About Right?"

► STRATEGY #14. DELIVER COMPELLING
EXECUTIVE PRESENTATIONS

Y our prospect's executives and
senior managers are busy people, overloaded with information, responsibility, commitments, and distractions. You've
asked for and been granted time to present your product or
service. Now the pressure's on. You have to deliver a clear,

143
△

concise, compelling, credible executive-level presentation to differentiate yourself and your product or service. If you perform well, you'll have gained the ear of the most powerful and influential people in your prospect's company.

Perhaps making a presentation to a roomful of powerful people is your least favorite part of the sales campaign. You're nervous; you find it hard to focus; you feel inadequate, out of your element.

Well, you're not alone. When sales professionals, even seasoned pros, come to me for help in building relationships with executives, they bring many woes:

▶ They have trouble differentiating themselves from the competition.

▶ They don't get the credibility they feel they deserve; executives become inaccessible, don't return phone calls, fail to influence key decisions.

▶ They feel that, no matter how hard they try, they cannot generate excitement or momentum in their presentations.

▶ They often find it a challenge to make their presentations work for them, even those requested by executives. As one fifteen-year veteran complained, "If we do a great job, the best that happens is that we get to stay in the evaluation. If we mess up at all — we're history."

If you have any of these same issues, stop and think: Do you start your presentation by talking about yourself, your company, your product or service? Perhaps what you need is a different approach.

> *"Where there is no difference, there is only indifference."*
>
> — LOUIS NIZER

Did you pick up the key words? Perform. Differentiate. Power. Influence. Understanding these concepts is the first step in making your presentation powerful and effective.

THE INVERTED PRESENTATION

What do people like to hear about? That's right: themselves. When you talk to an audience of executives, start by talking about them — their world, their company, themselves. The more knowledgeably and confidently you do this, the more credible you become. In fact, you will be judged by how closely your view of their business and industry matches theirs.

At the beginning of your presentation, think of yourself as a mirror, reflecting back to your audience what they already know. Once you have demonstrated your intelligence and insight by talking about things they are familiar with and can identify with and corroborate, they will believe you when, a few minutes later, you begin talking about the product or service you're selling.

> At the beginning of your presentation, think of yourself as a mirror, reflecting back to your audience what they already know.

I learned this reverse approach by getting myself into an uncomfortable situation. In 1990, at a first meeting in Manchester, England, with executives of a Scottish company, I started off with my usual polished slide presentation: "My company was founded in 1979. (Click.) We have offices in eight cities. (Click.) We have 100 employees. . . ."

"Hold on there, " said one of the executives. "Sorry to be so blunt, but we are more interested in hearing about how you propose to help us meet our business objectives. We want to be sure you know what those are, who we are, and what we do. We want to hear about your work with other companies like ours. If all that makes sense, then we will be willing to see your fancy slide show and learn all about you."

I turned on the lights, switched off the projector, and started talking. To be honest, I didn't know the company at all well enough to be considered a future business partner. But I knew a lot about the company's industry and a few of its competitors, suppliers, and customers. And that got me through the day. I learned a valuable lesson and never looked back.

145
△

Open your presentation by referring to events, challenges, or issues that your prospect and its industry have faced, are facing, and should expect to face. In particular:

▶ Choose one, two, or three topics to discuss with your audience — events, challenges, or issues that have recently affected their organization (see sample "Agenda," below). These could include a merger or an acquisition; a new product or a new geographic market; new government regulations or competitive pressures. Briefly discuss the background behind each issue and the effect it has had on the company. Subtly, not blatantly, lead them to recognize that had they invested in your product or service before these events, as other companies did, the outcome would have been better.

▶ Next, talk about a challenge they are now facing and how they might deal with it. Again, subtly position your offering to show the benefits of having your product or service in place now.

▶ Finally, talk about where their industry is headed and how they might benefit from your offering in the future.

If you're presenting early in the campaign, keep the benefits for them general but give specific examples of how you've helped other companies the prospect is familiar with. This will add to your credibility. In later presentations, however, talk more about specific benefits and their financial impact.

Agenda:
▶ Objectives for this meeting
▶ Your [prospect's] recent past
▶ Your [prospect's] current situation
▶ Your [prospect's] business outlook
▶ What we do and how we do it
▶ Other issues
▶ Next steps

Don't miss an opportunity to test your presentation with a coach or some other ally in the account. It's your best chance to corroborate your facts. When you go before the executives and talk about things they already know, you can stop occasionally and say, "Do I have

△

that about right?" — knowing full well, of course, that you are indeed right.

After you've spent ten or fifteen minutes discussing the prospect's history, challenges, and issues — and earned credibility for doing an accurate job of it — you may talk briefly about your company and your business solution. Be careful, however, not to "un-differentiate" yourself by going into your standard corporate pitch. Just use two or three slides telling them what your company does and how it does it. Be clear, compelling — and concise. Save the contract specifics — actual investments and returns — for later, after you've dramatically differentiated yourself.

Here are six things you must do to put together an effective inverted presentation:

1. Know Your Prospect

Before you ever get up in front of a team of executives, you must thoroughly understand their company, its industry, and, as much as possible, the individuals you're talking to. This is your situation assessment — the information you will have gathered when you scrutinized your prospect.

See chapter 11.

In addition to your insights into the past, present, and future, you should consider discussing the following points:

▶ From the buyer's perspective, how does your offering help it achieve its business plan?

One of our clients, a provider of web-based e-learning solutions, has to overcome the perception that its product is just a nice-to-have tool for the training department. The solution? Show how it can reduce travel expenses. This approach appeals to field operations execs and CFOs alike.

▶ What's the minimum financial return the buyer requires on products or services like yours?

▶ What has been the company's experience with products or services like yours? Has it been positive or negative? How does your approach differ?

▶ What is the buyer's usual relationship with suppliers? What does the buyer expect from suppliers?

When you use a strategic planning approach for executive presentations, you have a clearer picture of the situation as well as a better understanding of your audience. Here are other questions to answer before you face an executive team:

▶ Will any of the people there be connected in some way with your competition? Who gains if you're selected, and who loses? How do you find out? Winners seek to know the politics involved by negotiating access to key managers and executives while planning an executive presentation.

See chapters 9, 11, & 15.

▶ Will you have anyone in your audience who can stand up for you if you get into trouble? Can this person warn you ahead of time if someone is setting a trap for you, and if so, what that trap is?

Several years ago I consulted with a sales team that was preparing for an executive presentation. Concerned that we might be caught off guard by opponents of our plan, we asked an engineer on our team to get in touch with people he had worked with in the account. His contacts said yes, there could be trouble. They also told him who would raise objections and what they would be.

> Meticulous attention to detail is an asset. Your audience will be impressed by the effort you put into researching them.

Thus armed, we prepared an effective immunization, which we integrated into the first part of the presentation. The objections were never raised. But what would have been the result if the team had not made this effort to get detailed information about the attendees? Embarrassment and loss of credibility — exactly what you don't want as the outcome of an executive presentation.

Meticulous attention to detail is an asset. Your audience will be impressed by the effort you put into researching them. They will see clearly that you want to earn their business, and for many executives, that weighs heavily in their decision.

2. Understand the Objectives of the Meeting

Once you have completed a situation assessment of the meeting, think carefully about its objective. Or rather, think in terms of two objectives — yours and theirs. How will you formulate a presentation that encompasses both?

If the prospect asks for the meeting, its objective should be clear. Whatever it is, you should confirm it by phone or e-mail a few days before the meeting, or at least when the meeting starts.

What about your objective? If the presentation happens early in the process, your objective will probably include gaining or expanding your access to the executive team, or perhaps simply ensuring that you understand how the prospect will evaluate and decide. Later in the game, you may want validation that you understand the decision and approval process.

There's one objective above all that you want your presentation to achieve: differentiation from your competition. The inverted presentation approach goes a long way toward helping you gain that advantage, especially if your competitor doesn't use it.

3. Talk about Executive-Level Issues Only

No matter what you're selling, you must position it using business terms, financial measures of value, and the language used by your prospect and industry. You must show how your solution supports or, even better, advances the prospect's interests, whether it is departmental goals or the company's business objectives. If one person raises an operations-level issue, don't get into the nuts and bolts with him; you'll lose your momentum and your executive demeanor. Either frame an executive-level response or defer the answer — with the questioner's permission, of course — to a later, one-on-one discussion.

Avoid using jargon and buzzwords, which do little more than alienate you from your executive audience. Instead, talk about their products, customers, competitors, suppliers, and industry issues in company- and industry-specific language.

When you talk about what your company has accomplished with other clients in their marketplace, use specific testimonials and quotes from executives they know or whose names they will recognize. If you can give them actual numbers, so much the better: "Ray Herbst, the CFO of Global International, told us his company reduced customer attrition by 13 percent in just ten months using our solution." Be sure your numbers are accurate. Never give out this kind of information without the consent of those quoted or referred to, and be sure you're still on good terms with them — Ray may get a call from your current prospect.

More on references in chapter 21. ▶

4. DON'T PRESENT TO A MULTILEVEL AUDIENCE

Avoid having to present to audiences consisting of executives and people more than one organizational level below them. Tell your prospect early on that you require multiple sessions — one for executives, one for managers, and one for operations-level employees. This will probably cost you time and money, but it's more than worth it.

Here's why: You've established yourself as an expert in your prospect's business. You can talk to executives eye-to-eye and tell them, in their terms, how your offering can help the company achieve its business plan. But you have to maintain that posture; you have to keep being someone these executives can relate to and trust. Suddenly, though, they see you answering questions about (to them) insignificant details, talking shop with lower-level employees. What's an executive to think?

"I thought she was different. We talked about high-level issues."

"Why am I wasting my time listening to this petty stuff? I've got work to do."

"I'll delegate working with this sales rep. My staff can take care of the details."

△

When your objective is to build business relationships with the people who make the decisions and write the checks, this kind of thinking is very destructive.

On the other side, when you're presenting to executives and operations-level people at the same time, it's only natural to focus your attention on the execs. When you try to answer a minor question from a lower-level employee with the CEO sitting in the room, you may come across as condescending or arrogant. The employee may feel threatened and could later sabotage your deal.

5. Rehearse Your Presentation at Least Twice

Rule of thumb: Spend ten hours of preparation for each hour of presentation. Run-of-the-mill sales reps often smile when they hear this. They know they're far too experienced to waste that much time preparing. Why, they've been presenting for years.

The winners, sales pros who make the big bucks, smile too. But they smile because they know their secret's out.

Have you ever seen how the president rehearses for a news conference? Advisors take turns assuming the role of the most annoying, persistent, and inquisitive journalists who will be there. They probe for weaknesses with the

---

TACTIC: When you rehearse for an executive presentation with your team, have someone play the role of antagonist. Give him the responsibility of asking a wide range of tough, probing questions. Make sure you can answer them all confidently.

---

most difficult and embarrassing questions they can come up with, over and over, until all of the potential snares have been exposed.

This is how you should rehearse for executive presentations. Have your team hit you hard with all sorts of questions about your most troublesome customer, the recent departure of your CFO, deficiencies in your product, miscalculations in your ROI model, terms and conditions of your contract, and the like. Executives will test you. The way you perform under pressure may be one of their unwritten decision criteria. If your company can't deliver during the selling process, how will you possibly deliver after the sale?

Not long ago I was called to consult on a major software sales opportunity, just days before a crucial executive meeting. I was to make sure the two-day presentation went

---

Strategic Planning for Executive Presentations:

Situation Assessment: Details on the company, industry, issues, trends, competition, requirements, attendees, etc.

Objectives (ours): Differentiation, credibility, continued executive access, sponsorship

Objectives (theirs): To be determined

Strategy: "Inverted" presentation, rich with our insights about the prospect

Tactics: Research, advance test of presentation, rehearsal, perfect spelling, graphics, etc.

---

off without a hitch. As we rehearsed the demo two days before the event, the system crashed — not once, not twice, but three times. We worked frantically, got the problem resolved, and more: we arranged to have an engineer standing by during the presentation. It was a bomb with the fuse lit, but we made it go off prematurely — and harmlessly — by rehearsing.

But the real fun began when I sat with the sales team over dinner the night before the event. We did some role playing. I pretended I was the prospect's CFO coming to visit, and that I had been briefed by the competition about every possible weakness in my client's sales offering. It was a tough, frantic question-and-answer session. Even though it was just a rehearsal, I saw sweat pop out on the brow of at least one sales team member. So I pushed them even harder; I created impossible problems out of thin air, so the team could learn to control their reactions to unforeseen issues.

My thanks came during the actual presentation, in the form of a wink from the sales representative. One of the aggressive and potentially fatal questions I had surprised the team with in rehearsal was posed almost verbatim by someone we had tagged as an antagonist.

6. COMMUNICATE LIKE AN EXECUTIVE

Not the least of your concerns should be your professional style — how you come across as a communicator. There are mountains of books and programs on this subject, so I will offer a brief summation. You may have the best message, product, or proposal, but if you don't look like, sound like, and act like an executive, it will be an uphill battle all the way.

Look back at chapter 3 for more on this subject.

Executive style extends all the way from showing well-designed, perfectly spelled slides on faultless equipment to wearing high-quality clothes, driving your prospect to lunch in a high-quality automobile, and feeling completely comfortable around power. You have to feel like a million bucks to be comfortable asking for a million-dollar order — or to earn a million-dollar commission.

A TALE OF TWO VENDORS

Let me illustrate how much difference a single executive presentation can make. I was consulting for a CEO who was interested in hiring a large firm to improve his company's global sales capabilities. It was to be a very large project — too large, in fact, for my own firm to handle. I got approval from the CEO to consider only two firms. To spare injured feelings, let's call them DoRite Inc. and NoSweatCo Ltd.

Since my client's company was publicly traded, information about it was easily obtainable. In addition, some of its executives agreed to make themselves available to the competing vendors. I was, of course, willing to give the vendors any information about my client's requirements that they would need in order to create a proposal.

As you would expect, both vendors immediately asked to see the CEO. He agreed to meet with the president of each firm for an hour on consecutive days. I was to arrange the meetings and work with the vendors during their preparation.

Two weeks before the meeting, I got a call from two VPs and the account executive representing DoRite. They kept me on the phone for two hours. One of the most interesting things they asked about was the CEO's body language. How did he act when he was pleased, and when he wasn't?

I answered that the CEO's reactions were unusual. When he agreed with what was being said, he would frown. In fact, I told DoRite, when I first met him several years before, I thought he was displeased with something I said; only later did I discover that his was a frown of approval. It meant that he had already "bought" what you were saying and was thinking ahead about how it would apply to his situation.

When I got the expected call from NoSweatCo, it was rather perfunctory. They asked few questions. I was so uncomfortable with their lack of curiosity that I found myself coaching them on what they needed to know.

DoRite got the first meeting with the CEO. DoRite's president was there, along with his senior VP. I wish now that presentation had been videotaped. DoRite's president quickly showed how well he understood my client's company, as well as its industry, trends, challenges, opportunities, and best practices. Within only a few minutes, the CEO was frowning mightily. DoRite's president looked at me and gave me a knowing smile. It was easy traveling the rest of the way.

At the end of the hour, the CEO told me it was one of the best presentations he had ever seen. He was looking forward to meeting the other vendor, he said.

NoSweatCo's meeting, however, was a disaster. At one point its president made a big deal about inviting the CEO to a golf tournament he was sponsoring for other industry

CEOs. This time my client's frown was for real. The meeting ended abruptly after fifteen minutes, and as I walked the CEO back to his office, he said, "Stein, you're lucky I saw DoRite first. If I had started with NoSweatCo, there would be no project. We're going with DoRite. Schedule some time with me tomorrow so we can figure out how to sell this down through the organization."

NoSweatCo called me later that afternoon. "How did we do?" asked the account exec. As diplomatically as possible, I told him they had lost. "Why?" he asked. "The CEO hates golf," I replied.

I got to work a lot with DoRite. Its people understood well that knowledge and insight into the prospect's industry, business, and executives pays off in terms of credibility.

TACTIC: Make sure you know who will be attending the presentation. If there's someone in particular you want to attend, negotiate it well in advance. If that person is not available, offer to reschedule. Important: Get your prospect's word that if a key person who has agreed to be there does not show up, you will meet with that person later. Your negotiating position is probably stronger before the presentation.

"Scratch My Back & I'll Scratch Yours"

▶ STRATEGY #15. INVEST THE TIME TO BUILD BUSINESS RELATIONSHIPS

Y ou've often heard the phrase "win-win" used to describe a relationship or transaction that has mutual benefit. Does it still apply in the information age? Yes, more than ever. But win-win business relationships are getting harder to come by. A company looking for products or services has so many options now that buyers often lose sight of the benefits of maintaining long-term relationships, both business and personal, with suppliers. And we suppliers haven't helped the situation by letting buyers think and act that way.

Our buyers think that with all the alternatives in front of them they are in a good position. But when they wind up buying on price after beating up the vendors, they are just postdating the check they will eventually have to write. The old adage is true: Pay now or pay later.

It's our job to show the buyer there's business as well as personal value in investing in and maintaining a good relationship with us and our company. Winners master the skill of building win-win, mutually beneficial relationships with people in their accounts, leading to win-win relationships between their companies.

Building a relationship requires an investment of time by both parties. Face-to-face is best, but in today's selling environment, regular phone and e-mail communication can be effective as well.

THEIR COMPANY'S WIN

When we talk about win-win, what does your prospect win, other than the business benefit of using your products or services? If you've read this far, you'll know it's a thing called added value, which includes, among many other things,

- ▶ your interest in your customer's best interests,

- ▶ your knowledge, experience, and insight into his industry,

> *"Any business arrangement that is not profitable to the other person will in the end prove unprofitable for you. The bargain that yields mutual satisfaction is the only one that is apt to be repeated."*
> — B. C. FORBES

▶ your ability to understand his business plan and propose how you can help him achieve his goals and objectives, and

▶ your network of executives whose companies faced similar challenges that you helped them overcome.

And what should your company expect in return? More than just an order. If you've delivered personal value and earned credibility, consider yourself entitled to the second "win."

YOUR COMPANY'S WIN

The benefits of a win-win relationship for your company are things your customer can do to further your best interests, not just their own. These include

▶ giving your company leads to help you expand your business,

▶ guaranteeing you a baseline revenue stream that contributes to your company's business goals,

▶ agreeing to regular meetings between executives of both companies to foster a solid, long-lasting business partnership, and

▶ enhancing your competitive position by being an active proponent of your company to other buyers.

See chapter 21.

The closer the relationship, the better. Perhaps the buyer will lend you resources to help you develop products or services it will eventually need. Even better, it can give you the right of first refusal on all projects or purchases in your domain. If your company is small, your customer might even see fit to invest in it.

You can't have such a close relationship with every account. In fact, you may never have one that close. It depends on what you're selling, and in what marketplace, as well as how much value your customers think you can deliver. It also depends on how willing your own company is to form close partnerships and how assertively you pursue them. This is where you, personally, can make a difference.

Here's how: Early in the process — even as early as when you're first invited to join an evaluation — begin to negotiate the terms of a solid, long-term relationship. Remember what we said about establishing your right to qualify the buyer even as he's evaluating you? That's a good place to start. You'll either gain lasting respect as a businessperson or you'll get an unmistakable indication of what can only become a win-lose (you lose) relationship.

See chapter 9.

Sometimes you have to train your customer to seek win-win relationships — for example, by giving him something of value only when you get something of value in return. Suppose your prospect wants you to do a presentation for his research and development team; suppose also that you want to meet his CFO. Link these events together so you both get the value you're seeking. Do this again and again, and you'll eventually have a solid, mutually beneficial relationship.

This raises an interesting question for you as a sales professional: Do you, as a vendor, have rights?

VENDOR'S RIGHTS

As you pursue a win-win business relationship, consider claiming these rights for your company and yourself:

▶ If you can establish significant differences between your offering and that of your competitor, differences that the prospect agrees might have measurable benefit, you have the right to have those capabilities evaluated.

▶ If the evaluation process keeps you from contacting the prospect directly — as, for instance, when you're being evaluated by the buyer's consultant — or if a gatekeeper bars your access to executives who would directly benefit from your offering, you have the right to meet those people.

▶ Before naming your price, you have the right to gain an understanding of your prospect's business, its requirements,

and the contribution your offering could make toward achieving the company's business plan.

▶ You have the right to be treated ethically. I have found,
by the way, that the higher in the organization you sell, the
less people will lie to you. That alone is worth the effort of
getting in to see high-level executives.

▶ You have the right, and the duty to your company, to
walk away from an unqualified opportunity.

PERSONAL RELATIONSHIPS WITH KEY PEOPLE

Underlying a healthy company-to-company relationship you
will find sustainable, win-win personal relationships that
cross company boundaries. You can think of these relationships as having two personal components that you share
with your counterparts in the other company: (1) common
ground and (2) mutual benefit.

COMMON GROUND

As a sales professional, you are responsible for finding
the common ground between yourself and key people in
your account. What do I mean by "common ground"? The
possibilities are unlimited. It is any aspect of your lives that
you and the other person have in common — schooling,
military experience, past employers, hobbies, age of children, and so on. These are things you can relax and talk
about in personal terms.

While consulting for a large company in Japan, I was
invited to dinner by the vice president in charge of the division whose sales team I was coaching on a large, competitive opportunity. Having found out that I loved sushi, he took
me to an incredible subterranean restaurant in downtown
Tokyo. It was one of the finest meals I have ever had.

The only problem was that we had not established any
common ground on a personal level, and throughout dinner
my host was noticeably uncomfortable. That made two of us.

Finally, as we were finishing up, I saw a light go on in his eyes. "Dave-san, how old are you?"

"Tanaka-san, I am forty-nine years old," I said.

He was exuberant. Throwing his arms into the air, he said, "Dave-san, I am forty-nine years old, too!" He had found our common ground. Tanaka-san was finally comfortable.

I later learned, from someone schooled in Japanese culture, why Tanaka had been so uncomfortable. Since I was a consultant — an outsider, not easily positioned in Tanaka's age-oriented, hierarchical world — he just didn't know how to react to me. If I had been older than he, he would have had to show deference. Had I been younger, of course, Tanaka would have expected deference from me. Thus in another country did I begin to learn to think outside the box about common ground.

Here are a few of the many areas where you might find common ground with key executives in your client's company:

. . . assuming you've done the homework I talked about in chapter 11.

▶ where you grew up

▶ where you've lived

▶ schools attended

▶ military experience

▶ past jobs and careers

▶ unusual technical skills

▶ community service work

▶ contributions to charities

▶ reading Tom Clancy or Maeve Binchy

▶ watching *Seinfeld* reruns

▶ travel

▶ cuisine

▶ art or music appreciation

▶ hobbies, crafts, or sports

MUTUAL BENEFIT

The other component of a win-win personal-professional relationship, mutualism, is a bit more complex. The challenge here is to learn what the key people in your account have to gain personally from doing business with you. If this is a new subject for you, don't be alarmed. We aren't talking about anything unethical. All we are suggesting is that when people make decisions, they think along two lines at the same time, the rational and the emotional:

▶ Rational: Can the vendors deliver what they promise? When they promise? At the promised cost?

▶ Emotional: How will it affect me personally? Will it affect my work? Will it endanger my position?

Their Personal Perspective

A personal perspective in a business transaction? Sure. Every one of us has a personal win somewhere in mind as we make business decisions. This is not to say that our personal wins come first or that they should. If your personal goals are aligned with your company's, when your company gets what it wants, you'll get what you want.

Bad things happen to companies when people put their personal wins ahead of the companies' goals and objectives. I've seen it happen many, many times. An information technology manager, at great risk to her company, buys an unproven product using new technology rather than sticking with the proven product — so she can add a new skill to her résumé. A manager rejects a superior service because he's uncomfortable dealing with the "foreigners" who run it.

That said, I've found that many people who acknowledge having a personal win are reluctant to admit it to others for fear that their honest business decisions will appear self-serving. That's unfortunate, because these are legitimate personal goals in a professional setting:

▶ a raise

▶ a bonus

"Win" is a term I like to use in this context. It comes from Robert Miller's and Stephen Heiman's *Strategic Selling.*

163
△

- promotion
- recognition
- more influence
- access to power
- perks of all sorts
- an increased budget
- a challenging new assignment
- relocation to an exciting remote facility
- a new résumé entry for a successful initiative
- less pressure
- early retirement

TACTIC: As soon as possible, begin to learn the personal wins of the people who are part of the decision process. As your relationships with these people deepen, what they want often comes to the surface, especially in social settings. Earlier in the sales campaign, however, some gentle probing may be required.

Your Personal Perspective

What do you want out of the relationship? You need to make this clear, not only to yourself but also to the other person. It's more than just getting an order or winning a deal; to many sales reps, recognition in their marketplace is the holy grail; to others, friendships with influential executives, more influence in their own companies, time off to enjoy whopping commission checks, membership in the President's Club; most of all, a reputation as a winner.

Here are actions you should take as part of your standard sales approach:

- Identify your common ground with key people in the account.

▶ Identify people inside who could help you make the sale.

▶ Communicate your own personal wins.

▶ Seek to understand the other person's wins. This is best accomplished one-on-one outside the business setting — in a restaurant or in a social setting.

▶ Collaborate to attain your personal objectives ethically and honestly.

Do this, and you're well on your way to consistent, stellar performance.

DON'T FORGET YOUR OWN PEOPLE

Using their relationship-building skills, winners are those who have learned to surmount what is often the biggest obstacle to their success — people and practices within their own organizations. One of the services we offer clients is a group session with their top three to eight salespeople to determine best sales practices. The savvy pros I meet in these sessions tell me they are successful because they've figured out how to work their own organizations. They know how and with whom to build relationships to get the information, assistance, insights, and advice they need, even from people pursuing conflicting goals. They form win-win relationships with engineers, customer service reps, corporate attorneys, finance people, administrative assistants, key C-level executives — in short, anybody with common ground and potential mutual benefits.

> When you have a plan, it's much easier to enlist the support of others in your organization.

TACTIC: Ask yourself: With which people in your own company should you enhance your relationships? What's in it for them? What are the obstacles? Specifically, how will you accomplish it, and when?

One more thought: You can't strong-arm nonsalespeople in your company to help you win business. It never works.

See
chapter 19.

One way you can enlist their help, however, is to share your sales plan for the account where you need their help. Once you have convinced them that you are organized and have a strategy, that their role is important to the company's success, and that you will give them full credit for their contribution, barriers often dissolve.

The Stuff Winners Do

This part explores the wisdom of experienced sales pros who know what it takes to win, and keep winning, in today's competitive selling environment. The next four chapters will cover an arsenal of selling skills and behaviors, from the small but critically important details of selling to the broad range of networked resources you can tap into to win the deal.

Here is what you'll learn in this part of *How Winners Sell:*

- ▶ How keeping track of the details will raise your hit rate

- ▶ What you need to know about the competition in order to win, and where to get the information

- ▶ How to recruit and train an ally — inside the prospect's company! — to sell on your behalf

- ▶ How to lead your virtual sales team to victory

Keep reading, and remember: In sales, no detail is too small and no opportunity too large.

"Don't worry about him, he's just your competition."

The Devil Is in the Details

▶ STRATEGY #16. PAY METICULOUS ATTENTION TO DETAIL

Even though I cautioned you against too much detail in your strategy, you've surely figured out by now that, when appropriate, I embrace detail — lots of it. What do I mean by "when appropriate"? Simply that I try to balance the strategic with the tactical. I pay attention to the trees, but I don't let them block my view of the forest.

See
chapter 13.

169
△

When people hear the word "detail," they often think "trivial." It's a mistake to think this way. Attention to detail is important not only for function but for perception as well. People will pay top dollar for quality, and quality is seen in the details — the sophisticated engineering of a top-of-the-line Mercedes-Benz, the fit and stitching of a Savile Row suit, the attentions of a top-notch waiter in a fine restaurant.

The quality of your product or service should always be a selling point. And the attention you pay to executing the details of your sales plan translates into your prospect's perception of quality — the quality of your offering, of your company, and of you.

Your sales plan is as important to your sales success as a company's plans are to its future business success. How carefully and conscientiously are you, or the members of your sales team, executing the tactical details of your plan? For example:

▶ Do you know exactly what your best reference thinks about your company, or are you willing to wait until the day before your prospect visits her?

▶ Are you familiar with the finer points of your prospect's requirements, or are you missing the fact that training must be delivered in Spanish at two locations?

▶ Do you consider all your prospect's executives worth contacting, or can you ignore the opinions of the director of strategic planning?

▶ When your prospect asks you to provide ten references, do you figure that five is enough?

"I have always wanted to be somebody, but I see now I should have been more specific."

— LILY TOMLIN

▶ Do you investigate all of the objections your prospect states, or do you consider some of them unfounded and therefore not worth your time and attention?

▶ When your prospect asks how many customers you have using your product, can you respond with assurance, or is it not worth checking the facts?

▶ When meeting with your prospect, do you get directions in advance, verify them on a map, and arrive early enough to allow for traffic — or do you shrug and think, "So I'm a few minutes late"?

▶ Do you rehearse your presentations by having your team ask you tough questions, or do you trust to your ability to wing it?

I'm not suggesting that buyers always choose quality over price; I only wish it were so. But from working with winners, I do know that their customers, especially C-level executives, place value on your attention to detail — even when they're careless about details themselves. They want to know you won't overlook something that could make the difference between success and failure for their project, their career, or their company. By showing you care about the details, you gain credibility and earn their confidence.

When you're dealing with technical people or end users, you must be especially careful about details. I was recently hired to coach some sales engineers who had a problem: their prospects weren't signing contracts as expected. They kept leaving the details out of the design agreements specifying what the prospects would be acquiring. The prospects were getting more and more frustrated trying to get my clients to be more specific, to fulfill what the buyers saw as the providers' responsibility.

When you put yourself in the shoes of the buyer, I'm sure you'll agree that attention to detail is required behavior. So, as the seller, how do you cultivate the desired level of detail consciousness?

CHECKLISTS

The number-one tool that will help you pay more attention to detail is the simple checklist.

I saw my first checklist when I was eight — the one my mother pasted inside my steamer trunk the first time I went off to summer camp. You know: white socks, five pair; bathing suits, three; envelopes for letters home, twenty. Later, like you, I learned about to-do lists, recipes, sales call lists, business trip checklists, and so on. My wife uses checklists religiously when we travel to ensure that every detail of the trip goes smoothly.

But I never realized how critical the content and sequence of a checklist could be until I started piloting my own plane. There's a preflight checklist, of course, to ensure that all the parts of the plane are in place and working before getting airborne. There are also the fifteen other checklists I keep handy in flight — emergency checklists with ominous titles like "Emergency Landing Without Engine Power" and "Electric Fire in Flight." These lists, created and verified by the plane's manufacturer and the FAA, specify the sequence of steps that is most likely, in case of specific emergencies, to result in the survival of pilot and passengers. I've memorized some of these in their entirety; others, just the first few steps, to give me time to read the full list.

Checklists are critical for the successful completion of a flight of any length. A routine flight can become an emergency if routine checklists aren't followed. It's not hard to see that a checklist can be equally crucial to the successful outcome of a sales effort. It's the single best way to ensure that you have all the details covered.

Perhaps you're lucky enough to have a sales plan checklist that was compiled by your management or a predecessor. That's a good start. But the top sales pros develop, maintain, and improve their own checklists, based on their unique selling experiences. Checklists should be dynamic; they should reflect changes in customer buying trends, your company's procedures and processes, competitive influences,

△

and — perhaps most important — your personal strengths and weaknesses.

Bob DeGroot, president of Sales Training International, has posted a sales tactics checklist on his website (see the Resource pages at www.HowWinnersSell.com). I've adapted it here as a starting point for you. As you'll see, based on your unique selling situation, this list is neither complete nor necessarily in the proper sequence. In fact, the checklist should be customized for each sales opportunity, based on customer requirements and processes, your objectives, and your strategy.

I. BEFORE THE CALL

▶ Receive or generate sales lead.

See chapter 8.

▶ Perform preliminary research on your prospect's specific industry and business environment, issues, etc., and the person you will be calling. More detail is required here. This information should be captured in the situation assessment section of your account planning document.

▶ Determine first-call objectives for yourself and your prospect.

▶ Predetermine opening remarks that will establish your credibility.

See part 1.

II. FIRST CALL

▶ Make contact.

▶ Establish trust and rapport through questioning, based on what you already know about your prospect.

▶ Preliminarily qualify using several key criteria, i.e., buying plans, budget cycles, buyers, approvers, procurement and decision processes, etc.

▶ Confirm or discover prospect's (additional) critical business processes within your company's domain.

▶ Confirm or discover prospect's (additional) business plans to determine your potential contribution.

* The possibility that the prospect may decide not to buy from anybody

▶ Identify your actual and potential competitors (including "do nothing"*) and the prospect's perception of each.

▶ Identify potential generic objections (e.g., "We don't buy from small companies").

▶ Identify others in the prospect's organization who could benefit from what you sell and how they might benefit.

▶ Follow up with a (perfectly written) thank-you letter, highlighting any action items, agreements, or key points discussed.

III. FOLLOW-UP INTERVIEWS AND SALES CALLS

Chapter 11

▶ Scrutinize the prospect to produce a comprehensive situation assessment.

Chapter 9

▶ Further qualify based on your assessment.

Chapter 14

▶ Deliver executive presentation.

Chapter 9

▶ Obtain agreement on criteria, processes, time frames, and contacts for evaluation.

▶ Determine the value each buyer or decision maker could derive by using your offering. This information will be used in your proposal and the ROI it projects.

Chapter 13

▶ Determine your sales objective and commit it to paper or disk.

Chapter 13

▶ Determine your sales strategy and commit it to paper or disk.

► Continue recording tactics, events, and actions, including the ones in this list.

► Reserve time for members of your team and other key resources.

► Identify specific end users or consumers involved in project. Interview as required.

► Periodically solicit a restatement of buying or decision criteria and processes from buyers.

► Identify and arrange to meet other crucial players.

► Identify candidates to train as allies.   ◄ Chapter 18

IV. Additional and Continuing Tasks

► Schedule demonstrations, tests, pilot studies, and other required pre-purchase approvals. Assure that all crucial personnel attend.

► Arrange meetings or calls with other members of your team as appropriate.

► Stay in touch with key evaluators and decision makers (use Toole's Model).   ◄ Chapter 3

► Constantly update your research on your competition. Use sources inside and outside your prospect's company.

► Solicit objections from key evaluators, recommenders, decision makers, and approvers.

► Exchange any additional required data, specifications, drawings, documentation, etc., with the prospect

► Receive feedback from demonstrations, pilots, or other pre-approval events.

► Deliver on time and without fail on any commitments you or members of your team have promised.   ◄ These should be listed separately.

► Resolve any questions or issues that arise during the pre-approval processes.

► Develop product or service delivery phase-in plans.

► Exchange financial or credit information as necessary.

Chapter 21 ► Arrange reference calls or visits, making sure to brief your customer in advance.

► Provide your contract, licensing agreements, or other legal documentation promptly.

► Get any approvals you need from your own company.

V. PROPOSALS AND PRESENTATIONS

Appendix 1 ► Prepare ROI, making sure the return expected is within boundaries specified by your prospect.

► Prepare, pretest, and submit your business proposal.

► Present your proposal to key decision makers and buyers.

► Solicit affirmation that your proposal meets criteria.

► Engage in final negotiations.

► Get final approval on project/product/service budget.

► Ensure that the contract or agreement is signed and a letter of confirmation sent.

TACTIC: Key the checklist above (or more important, your version of the checklist) into your spreadsheet or sales automation tool. Use it to assure yourself that you will not be inadvertently missing any activities required to win the sales campaign.

Yes, there's a lot to keep track of — but this checklist is nowhere near as detailed as some I've seen. Think of it as just a framework on which you can construct your own, more detailed, custom-tailored sales campaign checklist. You'll need other checklists as well for transitioning from prospect to customer, maintaining existing accounts, and cultivating references.

See
chapter 21

Here are three important points about the list above:

1. Some of the items on this list will have checklists themselves, such as the executive presentation, and you should certainly create a list detailing all that must be done to create a proposal for the prospect.

2. Some of the items don't apply at all to your situation. You can remove these from your list — but first, make doubly sure they don't apply. If you lose an opportunity, says Bob DeGroot, it may be because of a required step you didn't have on your list. I'd hate for that to be a step you removed.

3. Every item on this checklist requires a resource — either you, a member of your team, or someone in your prospect's organization. When properly sequenced with actual dates, the list can be used not only to monitor the progress of your sales campaign but to ensure that you have the proper resources at hand when you need them.

I mentioned in chapter 13 that a spreadsheet is an effective tool for maintaining your checklist because you can easily resequence it by date, account, owner, or resource. It's also easy to add items as required. Leading sales automation software will manage this as well.

And here's a final word about details: When you've won a sale, don't forget to update your master checklist with all the items that were essential to winning that sale. Any one of these details might be just the crucial element in closing your next deal.

△

▶ Know Your Rival

▶ **STRATEGY #17. RAISE YOUR COMPETITIVE IQ**

Information about the enemy: the military calls it "intelligence." The government considers it important enough to assign intelligence gathering to thirteen different agencies. And now we know, with newfound painful awareness, the result of not having timely, accurate, and comprehensive military intelligence.

Do you have timely, accurate, and comprehensive intelligence about your competition? Okay, it's not as weighty a concern as the military kind, but it can play a major role in the success of your sales campaign, perhaps even your company. Back in chapter 7, I talked about getting into a competitive state of mind as an essential component of surviving in a hypercompetitive business world. In order to thrive, you'll have to raise your level of competitive intelligence. You will need to understand your competitor's capabilities and behaviors — not just rival companies but the sales professionals you go head to head with — so you can anticipate their future actions and plan more effective sales campaigns to counter them.

In this chapter I'll discuss the three levels of competitive information that are available to you as a sales professional. The key word here is "available." Many of you just don't get enough information about competitors to support successful sales planning and execution — and it's generally not your fault. Few companies do what it takes to gather, analyze, and disseminate competitive information effectively, on time, and in a format that's useful for sales professionals. It costs money, and a lot of companies are too small to afford it. Many companies that can afford it don't understand the importance of competitive intelligence. In either case, to be a winner, you may have no choice but to take matters into your own hands.

What follows includes a lot of detail, but don't worry — you probably won't need to dig out all three levels of information about every possible competitor. Your business situation is uniquely yours. You may compete against the same three or four companies for every deal; your contracts may be $50,000 or $50 million; you may win more than you lose.

"There is nothing more exhilarating than to be shot at without result."

— **Winston Churchill**

All you really need to do is design your intelligence-gathering activities to suit your situation.

When you're analyzing and positioning against your competitor, objectivity is important. Just as we do with self-assessment, few of us start out being entirely objective about competitors. Some of them we overestimate; others we underestimate, which is even more dangerous. Learn to gauge the true measure of your competition, and you'll plan your sales campaigns more effectively.

Failure to Disseminate

A few years ago, one of my clients was losing nine out of every ten deals to one tough competitor. The CEO and VP of sales assigned ten people to help me turn the situation around and gave me access to sales reps, product experts, cost accountants, marketing people, and administrative help.

Most important, they gave me the cooperation of all their field sales executives. These people had years of experience competing with their number-one nemesis, but the company had never systematically compiled and shared this vast store of knowledge.

Three weeks later, we had produced a competitive playbook that gave every sales rep worldwide an amazing volume of high-quality Level 1, 2, and 3 information, along with a detailed, two-by-five-foot map of the competitor's winning sales process. In one way we were lucky: the competitor had strong sales leadership at the corporate level, so most of their field personnel followed their recommendations on how to beat us. Because there was little variation in their approach, we could anticipate their every move. We found it easy to make specific recommendations every step along the way when we competed against them.

That was the beginning of the end for that competitor. Not only did my client lose no more business to them, but the competitor eventually lost the support of the press, the industry, securities analysts, their partners, and their own people. Bankruptcy followed a few years later.

LEVELS OF COMPETITIVE INTELLIGENCE

Now we'll take a closer look at the three levels of competitive information you'll need in order to design effective sales strategies and tactics. Within each level, I'll give examples for each of several different categories of information, along with questions you can ask yourself (or others) in order to use that information to best advantage, ending up with likely sources for specific kinds of information.

LEVELS OF COMPETITIVE INFORMATION

Level	Content Area	Availability	Value to You
1	Competitor's company	Easy	Low
2	Competitor's product/service	Strengths: Easy	Moderate
		Weaknesses: Difficult	Substantial
3	Competitor's sales execution: team or individual	Continuing effort	Very high

Earlier in *How Winners Sell*, I wrote about how much easier it is to get information about public-company prospects than about private companies. The same holds true for Level 1 and some Level 2 information about your competitors. In fact, the real challenge is that there's often too much. It takes time and effort to sort through this infoglut and find the nuggets that tell us how best to compete.

Level 3 information, however, is different. It's equally elusive for both public and private companies. And it's the kind of information winners go looking for: intelligence on the competition's sales strategies and tactics.

LEVEL 1: COMPANY INFORMATION

Level 1 information is information about your competitor's company that is generally available, often because the company publicizes itself. It includes:

▶ Company background. Is it a young company or a well-established one? What is its reputation? What background information is it likely to highlight or to hide?

▶ Annual revenues and other financial information. Is your competitor making or losing money? Expanding or shrinking? Gaining or losing market share? Do your prospect's decision criteria include financial viability? If so, are you at a competitive advantage or disadvantage?

▶ Officers, managers, private investors. Are they seasoned or green? Where did they come from? How long have they been there? What are their backgrounds — finance, engineering, sales? Who in your prospect's company might be turned on or turned off by a call from your competitor's executive team?

▶ Key customers, partners, competitors, industries served. Do your competitors brag about marquee-name accounts? Are they small, but with big, stable business partners? Are they credible experts in the industry, or are they taking the bayou approach?

See chapter 6.

▶ Job openings. These may signal new product development (Level 2) or regional or global expansion. If they're not advertising job openings in an expanding market, your competitors may be experiencing or anticipating a downturn in business. That could greatly impact their ability to support their customers.

▶ Key business strategies, outlook, and significant changes or events. Are your competitors pursuing new markets or geographies? Are they on an acquisition binge, or are they divesting unprofitable business units? What impact will any of these factors have on the prospect? Will this be good news or bad news for you?

▶ Key corporate messages, such as 100 percent customer satisfaction, highest quality, or quickest time to value. If "quality and commitment of vendor personnel" is a decision criterion set forth by your prospect, and your competitor is

△

listed in *Fortune* magazine's "Best Companies to Work For" list, you may be at a disadvantage.

▶ How large is your competitor's sales organization, and how is it structured? Does your competitor sell directly, or through alternate channels?

Where to get Level 1 information:

▶ Your competitor's own website. That's where you'll get what the company wants to portray to its customers, investors, employees, the press, and even its competitors.

▶ Government filings, such as 10-Qs, 10-Ks, proxy statements, and statements of ownership. By now you know that www.freeedgar.com is a reliable source of financial information for public companies.

▶ Securities and industry analyst reports. Most of what I said earlier about your prospects is applicable to your competitors as well. Make sure you're up-to-date on what key analysts are saying about your competitor and you. Positive analyst reports are among the most believable tools that salespeople can use in their campaigns; they are considered to be unbiased, written by informed experts.

This is a good
time to reread
part 1.

▶ Press releases, corporate newsletters, magazine articles. If your company subscribes to LexisNexis or another subscription service, you're in good shape. If not, you'll have to bone up on your Internet search skills to keep up with competitive Level 1 information.

▶ Press kits and investor relations packets.

▶ Vendor listings in online and other catalogs, as well as your competitor's business partners' sites.

▶ Internet investor bulletin boards. Although these messages are rife with rumor and the hyping of other stocks and investor services, I have, over the years, gotten many leads as to what was really going on within a company from messages posted on these boards.

▶ Services and sites designed specifically for gathering and interpreting competitive intelligence.

LEVEL 2: PRODUCT OR SERVICE INFORMATION

There are two categories of information about your competitor's products and services: (1) information that is generally available, and (2) information that is intentionally made difficult to uncover.

Examples of generally available product and service offering information:

▶ Names of products and services, along with general descriptions, specifications, capabilities, and (of course) strengths. This information is helpful in preliminarily qualifying the opportunity.

▶ Universal benefits associated with the product or service.

▶ Product or service availability by geography, date, language, color, etc.

▶ New product or service introductions, or upgrades or enhancements to existing products. One of my clients collected three years' worth of new-product announcements their competitor had issued and compared them, in table format, to what was actually delivered. The table became a potent competitive sales tool.

Here's where to get generally available Level 2 product and service offering information:

▶ Company websites under "What We Do," "Products," or "Services"

▶ Press releases, magazine articles, testimonials, case studies, etc.

▶ Product brochures requested by mail or picked up at trade shows

▶ Vendor listings in online and other catalogs, as well the competitor's partners' sites

▶ Comparisons done by magazines, by independent organizations, or by securities or industry analysts.

Examples of Level 2 information with limited availability:

▶ Product deficiencies, including quality, design, or functional limitations. Needless to say, this is valuable competitive information.

▶ Service offering limitations. For example, if a full-service law firm doesn't have attorneys experienced in trusts and estates, they will be at a disadvantage when competing for the business of certain prospective clients.

▶ Historical actual selling price. If you're involved in a sales campaign that will ultimately come down to price, you can save yourself and your company a lot of money if you know in advance how low your competitor will go. You may even decide it's not worth getting involved.

▶ Where is the product in its life cycle? How much longer will the current product be offered, serviced, or supported? When was it introduced? What technology or intellectual property is it built on?

▶ Announcements of new products. For competitive reasons as well as keeping sales volumes consistent on existing products, companies often don't publicly announce new products.

▶ Terms and conditions of sale. Does your competitor have a complex, entirely self-serving contract that customers or clients must sign?

Where to get Level 2 information with limited availability:

▶ Customers of yours who have used your competitor's products or services previously or at another company. One sales team I worked with a few years ago found out that a vice president who had left the prospect's company two years before was now working at another company that was having a bad experience with the competitor's product. That executive called former colleagues to warn them off the product.

▶ Internet investor bulletin board postings (see above).

▶ Usenet newsgroup postings on the Internet. These might include job postings for new products, as well as complaints, comparisons, and other insights. (You can find the latest information about accessing these sites on the Resources pages at www.HowWinnersSell.com.)

▶ User community or group meetings. Perhaps a business partner, friend, reporter, analyst, or customer of yours has attended or will attend one of these sessions, in many of which issues are aired.

▶ Competitive win-backs or replacements. Winning back a lost customer or replacing your competitor's product or service often puts you in a position to learn about what your competitor did or did not deliver. If it is not propri- etary, you may be able to get your hands on your competitor's proposal, as well as on other documentation, such as status reports or internal communications about problems.

▶ Other websites. To give my clients a "heads up" about products or services their competitors may be developing, I've used the U.S. Government Patent and Trademark Office website: www.uspto.gov. The same holds true for new In- ternet domain names that may have been registered in ad- vance of product or service announcements. You can check with your company's webmaster for help or log onto www.HowWinnersSell.com for further information.

LEVEL 3: HOW YOUR COMPETITOR SELLS

Many of the world's largest and most successful companies provide their sales reps with lots of Level 2 information and even more Level 1 information online and in binders and CDs handed out at sales meetings. But rarely do these compa- nies provide a competitive playbook, with action-by-action instructions for beating specific competitors or individuals. This intelligence would be especially useful, because sales reps typically run up against the same people time after time but know very little about them.

Can you imagine boxers, football players, or tennis pros not knowing everything about their opponents before the big game or match? In the realm of professional sports, that's not even an option. Videotapes recorded from every conceivable angle are reviewed, consultants are brought in, and a game plan is constructed.

Level 3 information is all about your competition's sales strategy and execution. It's about how the sales rep who goes head to head with you plays the game. Gathering, analyzing, maintaining, and distributing Level 3 information is not easy. It takes time, resources, motivation, and money from corporate executives, department heads, and individuals.

In one company I worked with, we created a simple online bulletin board where every sales rep, no matter where in the world he worked, was required to post Level 3 information about his two main competitors in every active campaign. Every month, a competitive analyst would look for common elements, strategies, and tactics, data that would indicate policy coming down from corporate or regional management. Then they would recommend ways for our field reps to defeat them.

There's another good reason to set up this sort of intelligence system: When your high-achieving sales rep competitor becomes a sales manager, he will direct his sales force to use the same strategies and tactics he found successful against you. If you know how he sold as a rep, you'll be ready when his reps go up against yours.

By the same token, a canny competitor might use the same intelligence tool against you. If you could know what was in your competitor's win/loss analysis, you'd be better equipped to compete. You're probably not on the distribution list for this information, though, so you'll have to do some sleuthing. Here are some questions about your competitor's methods, questions you should be trying to answer if you intend to outsell your competition and win the big sale.

▶ What is your counterpart's typical sales process? Has her company adapted any of the well-known methodologies? If so, you can anticipate her approach.

▶ Does she wrestle for control of the evaluation process or decision criteria? Or is she more passive, letting the prospect steer the bus?

▶ Who does she typically call on in accounts? Finance, manufacturing, marketing, or sales? Users, managers, or board members?

▶ How is she measured and compensated? Is she on salary plus small bonuses or a highly leveraged (and motivating) commission plan?

How a rep is compensated is often a factor in how aggressively she sells.

▶ What is your win/loss ratio against her? What is your company's record against hers?

▶ How much information does she typically gather on her prospects? Is she well informed, bartering that information for access and more information, or are you in a more credible and valuable position through your knowledge and insight?

▶ What sales strategies does she typically use? What does she count on to win? This may or may not relate to the messages her company broadcasts to the marketplace. For example, her company may depend on its name recognition and size, but she may be a strong relationship builder.

▶ Why does she win? Why does she lose?

▶ What is her view toward you and your company? What does she say about you to your prospects? If your competitor is first in the door with every bit of bad news about your company, you'll need to immunize your prospects in advance. Follow the advice of Andrew V. Mason, M.D.: "Admit your errors before someone else exaggerates them." Why? Because you'll build your prospect's trust while depriving your competitor of a tactical victory. Even better: if it's early in the sales campaign, you'll set a barrier against negative selling, which might put a crimp in your competitor's tactics.

▶ In the past, what tactics have you used that were effective against her?

▶ Who or what does she consider her biggest competitive threat? It may not be you — in which case, you may be able to progress quite far in your campaign before you're taken seriously.

▶ Does she always seem to know and provide your prospects with the names of your least-satisfied clients? If so, what are you going to do about it?

▶ Does she keep her promises? Does she lie? Does she misrepresent her product, service, or company capabilities? Or is she highly principled, counting on her integrity as an advantage?

▶ What does she do if (or when) she panics? Does she go over the decision maker's head? Drop her price? Call in her manager? Negative sell against you?

▶ How much does she know about the industry she's selling into? If the answer is little or nothing, you have the beginnings of a competitive advantage.

▶ How long have she and her team been employed by her company? Does she have a solid track record, or has she been doing a lot of job hopping, perhaps leaving unhappy customers behind?

▶ When she's winning and trying to speed up the process, what incentives does she offer the prospect to get the deal closed? Discounts? Free service? "Platinum customer status"? How might you dilute the value of what she's offering?

▶ Does your competitor always ask for the first or the last slot for her presentations? How might you take advantage of this behavior?

▶ When your competitor loses, what's the reason? If she cannot answer this question objectively, if instead she blames her losses on everything and everyone but herself, you might be able to win against her again and again the same way. I've seen it happen many times.

▶ What does your competitor do to hide weaknesses in her product, service, or company? How might you set her up for embarrassment or failure?

Where to get Level 3 information:

▶ Attend the next bidder's conference and learn the name of the person you're competing against.

▶ Ask someone you're on good terms with in your prospect's company to talk to you about the value you're providing during their evaluation. Lead into some questions about your opponents.

▶ Call someone who used to work with your competitor but is now working for someone else. If you work within an industry niche, as I suggest you should, you'll invariably hear about personnel changes like this. Not only that, you'll probably be attending industry association meetings, where you'll have opportunities to meet or find out about your competition.

▶ Call up any recruiters you've worked with. They may know your competitors personally. If not, they may know someone who does.

TACTIC: Want to try a real "get out of your comfort zone" ploy? Call up your competitor and introduce yourself. Engage him in conversation. Talk about your successes and expectations for further success. Ask how he's doing. You might get a sense of his confidence, style, intelligence, and temperament. Maybe you'll even shake him up a bit.

▶ At your own company's sales meetings, discuss specific competitors on breaks and after hours. Don't trust your memory; take notes. In fact, suggest that a rep at each future meeting present Level 3 information about one competitor.

191
△

Ask a sales rep from another vendor who serves the same industry but does not compete with you.

▶ Get access to your own company's win/loss reports. With any luck, these will have been done by an impartial third party who knew what to ask, and whom. If that's the case, there's important Level 3 information just waiting to be brought to light.

Maintaining enough competitive intelligence to make a difference is a task that never ends. That's why you have to get into a competitive state of mind.

The winners will tell you you don't have much choice.

Chapter 18

►"Hold On While I Close My Door"

► STRATEGY #18. ENLIST AND TRAIN AN INFLUENTIAL ALLY

"**S**o, in conclusion," you say, "I want to thank all of you members of the evaluation team for giving my company the opportunity of presenting today. I trust you see clearly, as I do, that we can deliver a cost-effective, proven solution to the challenges you are facing today and be there with you as you meet and exceed your future business goals and objectives."

193
△

You close your briefcase, apply a practiced, confident smile to your face, and head out the conference room door. You figure it's all over but the shouting and the signing, right?

Wrong. What happens next is often the difference between winning and losing a deal.

SCENARIO ONE

"So what do you think about MacGregor's offering?" asks the evaluation team leader, seconds after the door closes behind you.

Immediately there's a flurry of tough questions — "What were the names of those three companies that complained about MacGregor's service?" "What about MacGregor's financial troubles?" "What was the reason for all those recent management changes?" — all concerning nonpublic information that has been planted by one of your competitors.

More questions arise. The debate heats up. Those favoring MacGregor's offering are up against tough opposition. Caught off-guard, unprepared for this scuffle, they are reluctant to take a stand.

Were you able to watch this discussion unfold, you would feel the deal slipping from your grasp. Who have you trained to sell on your behalf when you aren't there? Nobody.

SCENARIO TWO

"So what do you think about MacGregor's offering?" asks the evaluation team leader as the door closes behind you.

Immediately there's a flurry of tough questions — "What were the names of those three companies that complained about MacGregor's service?" "What about MacGregor's finan-

> "The absent are never without fault. Nor the present without excuse."
>
> — BENJAMIN FRANKLIN

cial troubles?" "What was the reason for all those recent management changes?" — all concerning nonpublic information that has been planted by one of your competitors.

More questions arise. The debate heats up. Those favoring MacGregor's offering are up against tough opposition. But one team member, Charlotte, is quietly taking it all in. She even seems to be holding back a smile.

She's saying to herself: "This is exactly what he told me would happen. Let's just wait a few more minutes, until all the objections have been raised and the battle lines have been drawn. Then I'll respond to them, one at a time. . . ."

EXTRA EYES AND EARS

Who is this person preparing to help your company, even in your absence? She's a project team member you've carefully recruited and trained to sell on your behalf when you're not there. About two months ago, you saw this bright, respected, potentially influential person in your prospect's finance department and thought she might make a good ally. You knew it would take some time, but building a relationship with her would give you an extra set of eyes and ears when and where you most needed them, and a mouth to speak for you when you were elsewhere.

You saw that Charlotte had an open mind, no apparent biases, and the tendency to ask probing but fair questions about what you were selling. She told you exactly how your offering did or did not meet the company's decision criteria, as she saw it. Impressed with her intelligence and insight, you sought to find out more about her, her role in the company, and how her colleagues and superiors saw her.

You quickly discovered that Charlotte was ambitious; she wanted to be on the fast track up the corporate ladder. So you spent most of the first month giving her your observations about who had the most influence in her company and how they might help her advancement. She took your advice seriously and soon found she was better able to use her own influence to her company's benefit, and her own.

In a professional way, you taught her how to analyze the capabilities of the vendors competing for her company's business, and to understand what was real and what was hype. Without getting specific, you provided enough general information to keep her from steering her company toward an offering that was not what it was purported to be. She soon realized that you were giving her information and insight that would make her quite valuable to the rest of her team.

You also sent Charlotte e-mails containing news articles, press releases, and other items of potential interest to her and the executives at her company. You took the time to add your own comments and observations on the effects this news would have on her company and its industry, competitors, and customers. As a result, Charlotte found herself becoming more knowledgeable and confident, venturing further into discussions of business and strategy with her boss.

Not least, you spent four or five weeks training Charlotte on two important aspects of selling: objection handling and timing. You talked about some of the concerns you knew would be raised by your competitors and by nonbelievers in her company. You gave her copies of analysts' financial reports and projections, talked frankly and in detail about five accounts that had complained about your company, what your company was doing to remedy the problems, and why they would not recur. You showed her how to deal with those concerns effectively — to turn the objections into valid reasons to buy from your company. Not least, you spoke frankly about the risks Charlotte would run by taking sides in an evaluation like this; you promised her you would do everything possible to keep her from being caught off-guard.

INTERESTS IN COMMON

Why did you and Charlotte both see fit to form an alliance? Your motives were plain, and you gave Charlotte valid and honorable reasons to help your cause. But behind these reasons was a more basic fact: Charlotte's professional and personal wins were linked with yours.

Charlotte wanted her colleagues to see her as knowledgeable, politically astute, promoting the company's interests. She hoped her contribution to the project would boost
her career, and you provided her some of the fuel she would
need to get that boost.

You wanted to win this business for your company, and
to have an ally who was clearly headed up the ladder, where
she would be helpful to you in the future. She showed you
that she trusted you; once, when you called on the phone,
she said, "Hold on a second while I close my door." After she
gave you some information that would help you improve
your position, you asked her directly to help you win. And
she did.

TACTIC: Pick someone in each of your accounts who might become an
ally. Make sure this person exhibits the skills, behaviors, and traits displayed
by "Charlotte" in the story above. And remember: when you train someone to sell on your behalf, make sure he's not only committed to helping
you win but has the skills to help effectively.

ALLIES, COACHES, AND SUPPORTERS

I like to distinguish among three types of people inside the
company you're selling to who can help you promote your
offering:

▶ An *ally* is a person who will sell on your behalf. In
   the above scenario, Charlotte is your ally.

▶ A *coach* will provide information that will help you
   win, but will not actively and openly favor you.

▶ A *supporter* will vote for you, but will avoid doing
   anything to give you an advantage before the vote
   takes place.

The same classification applies to your competitors, of
course. Part of your continuing qualification process should

be to learn the names, responsibilities, and influence of not only your allies, coaches, and supporters but those who will back your competitors.

Can you win without an ally? In some cases, yes. But in most cases, if you win without having recruited and trained an ally, you probably had one — you just weren't aware of it.

Chapter

Team Up to Win

STRATEGY #19. HARNESS THE POWER OF YOUR VIRTUAL SALES TEAM

U p to now, we've spent most of our time talking about managing yourself, your sales campaign, and your prospect, with particular attention to the skills, attitudes, and behaviors needed to win the big sale. Now it's time to acknowledge the fact that winning sales is not an individual activity but a group or team pursuit.

199
△

In the introduction we discussed some of the reasons behind the challenges facing sales professionals today. I mentioned two crucial factors in consistently winning business: differentiation and credibility. In today's playing field, it's getting harder and harder to make your offering seem different from all the others, or to earn credibility at the executive level.

> In today's playing field, it's getting harder and harder to make your offering seem different from all the others, or to earn credibility at the executive level.

The fact is that most competing products and services do what they're intended to do. Few offerings fail to perform, few perform markedly better than the rest. Because so many products and services compete for a limited number of buyers, suppliers advertise that they can do everything their competitors can do, only faster, cheaper, more effectively. They're all singing that song from *Annie Get Your Gun*: "Anything You Can Do, I Can Do Better."

How can companies differentiate themselves from all the others? By building in extra features; by backing what they're selling with top-notch customer service; by making their products and services more complex. However, this approach to differentiation goes well beyond what even the most articulate, charismatic salesperson can communicate. Explaining and managing that complexity to the prospect requires the help of specialists, technicians, and other experts. And that means taking a team approach to selling.

Team selling isn't new. Its growth has been spurred not only by the proliferation and complexity of goods and services but by many other trends over the years: multiple and diverse buying influences, user empowerment in organizations, globalization, commoditization, economic uncertainty,

> *"Individuals play the game, but teams win championships."*
> — Anonymous

and companies springing up and crashing down almost randomly. It all adds up to a hard reality: we can't do all the selling alone.

THE COMPANY TEAM

The team we're going to talk about is not just the people who work directly for or with you. It's much broader than that. In effect, your sales team includes people inside and outside your organization, independent technicians and professionals, people in other organizations, even people in other industries. As a sales professional charged with harnessing the skills and energy of this diverse crew of workers — some of whom aren't even aware they're on your team — you are, in effect, the CEO of an outfit we'll call "Virtual Sales Team Inc." And VST's mission is to deliver to your real company the revenue it needs to achieve its business plan.

Who's on your virtual sales team? The roster can include (inside your real company) executives, customer support reps, on-site service or delivery personnel, engineers, designers, developers, domain experts, cost accountants, marketing personnel, consultants, suppliers with complimentary products, other sales reps within your own company, attorneys, one or more current customers, and even consultants who can give you insight into how to win the business.

But Virtual Sales Team Inc. encompasses much more than just your inside team. Remember what we said in the first three parts about cultivating relationships and gaining knowledge inside the company you're selling to? Think of your virtual corporation as including the prospect's team — the evaluation committee, decision makers, steering committees, executives, users, middle management, technical approvers, purchasing and human resources personnel, finance and legal people, external consultants, administrative assistants, and IT people. Yes, that's right, they're on the other side of the bargaining table — but with knowledge, insight, a professional attitude, and people skills, you can enlist them in support of your cause.

THE MAKING OF A WINNING TEAM

As CEO of Virtual Sales Team Inc., you've got an awesome challenge ahead of you. First of all, most of your team members are not under your direct authority or supervision. You have to understand the knowledge, skills, attitudes, and behaviors of all the sales resources available to you. You'll need well-honed relationship-building skills to get these team members lined up behind you and focused on your common purpose. If, for example, you need an expert to tell your prospect how your company services its customers, but the person available for that task gets defensive and rude when questioned, you have some work to do. You'll need to coach that person before the meeting, or if that fails, bring in someone else. Don't leave it up to chance.

Like any good supervisor, you must learn to depend on other people to achieve your goals. With this challenge in mind, how can you better manage your virtual sales team? According to internationally recognized sales expert Steve Waterhouse, president of Waterhouse Group, team selling will succeed if the following components are part of your sales process:

▶ Effective communication. Make sure everybody gets the word early. You can't imagine how often this doesn't happen. (Heading out the door on Friday afternoon, the sales rep says to a sales support person, "By the way, we've got a presentation in Duluth Monday morning. Have a nice weekend." What's his problem? Is he grossly incompetent, operating without a plan, or is he simply a poor communicator?)

▶ Team understanding of the mission. Every member of the virtual sales team must be aware of exactly what your objective is: what you are committing to sell, when you are going to sell it, and for how much. Each team member should also understand that every tactic has an objective of its own.

▶ A clear understanding of each member's role. Nothing is more embarrassing than asking the prospect the same question twice because Smith didn't check with Jones. More on this later.

▶ Planning. Back in chapter 13 we talked about outlining your tactical plan in a spreadsheet or sales automation application. You might also find project management software useful if you're working a complex deal with a lot of resources, tasks, and critical deadlines. Whatever planning tools you use, be sure to keep your team members well informed.

▶ Smart use of your team members' knowledge and skills. Know what all team members are capable of, and use these assets at appropriate times. Need to get one of your prospect's decision makers on your side? Bring in your company's cost accountant to help her with financial justification. Or perhaps a strategically timed visit from your well-known, world-class expert would get the attention of one of your prospect's key executives.

▶ Good leadership. When you earn the prospect's confidence by establishing your competence and credibility, you're well on your way to making the sale. In the same way, when you earn your team's trust with strong, fair leadership, they will buy into your plan and follow your vision to sales success.

▶ Focus. If you follow my sales planning recommendations in chapter 13 and communicate the plan to all team members, focus will not become an issue. Your sales team will commit to a coordinated effort that makes winning the deal an achievable goal.

▶ Support and motivation of team members. This one takes work, empathy, and an understanding of how your company's departments function. Except for your sales support staff, most of your team members have other responsibilities, of which helping to win sales is not high priority. In fact, some of the people who may be essential to your success may be reluctant to help you because they believe it will increase their risk or their workload.

Some companies give sales award trips and other recognition to nonsales staff who have helped win business. My hat goes off to these firms. This is a great motivator, as well as a chance for engineering, delivery, finance, and other personnel to see where revenues that pay for their work come from. At presidents' clubs presentations, again and again I've seen sales professionals lavish more attention on those who helped them win than on other sales reps. That's smart selling.

▶ Active participation and collaboration. Even though the responsibility for winning or losing the sale falls on you, all team members need to feel they are part of a continuing collaboration. Invite and encourage their participation in brainstorming sessions, information gathering, and meeting prospects' requirements.

▶ Integrity. Showing leadership, vision, and guts will gain you the trust and support of others. Make promises you can't keep or lie to your team or your prospect, and you'll go it alone.

▶ Conflict resolution. Yes, you're the owner of that sales campaign, but this doesn't mean you can dictate. Be ready for the conflicts that are sure to arise with members of your team. How will you deal with them? One way to keep conflicts from derailing a sales campaign is to recruit an executive as a sponsor early in the game — one whose trust you will win with your leadership skills and competence, and who will back you in the end.

Conflicts between team members will arise from time to time. Personal and professional differences make them inevitable — differences in job descriptions, business knowledge, experience, incentive plans, geographic locations, schedules, personalities, outside commitments, and communications style, to name but a few.

The most common conflict is perhaps between those who sell and those who have to deliver, install, or implement. I've seen this happen again and again. Sales complains that production or service managers are stalling, refusing to sign off on a deal that would put them over quota. Managers responsible for manufacturing the product or delivering the service complain that sales overpromises, leaving them to face angry customers. The lack of trust can bleed over into customer meetings and presentations, giving prospects the impression that the company can't get its act together and perhaps can't be relied on to meet its commitments.

What can you do about it? Building trust and support will take time, but it can be done. The best solution is to review and apply Steve Waterhouse's critical components — the items you just read. And the best place to start applying them is in team meetings, where planning and communication take a front seat.

DISCOVERY

Early in the campaign, the important thing is to get all your team members on the same page, share available knowledge, and plan ways to gather other required information. The first few meetings should be formal, with a printed agenda, including clear goals and time constraints (showing respect for team members' time). Their objective is to determine the prospect's requirements, based on research, preliminary conversations, and even RFPs, and what the best way is to find out what the prospect isn't telling you, or perhaps doesn't know, about his company's business needs. This process is called "discovery."

It's useful during discovery to categorize by type the information you need to collect. But it's also helpful to think in terms of which team member is in the best position to get it; people who don't have "sales" on their business card are often the most effective intelligence operatives.

Remember Strategy #12? That's right: Know what your customer is buying before you begin selling. When you're meeting with the prospect early in the discovery phase of your campaign, it's better to ask questions than to present. Try to bring along a business, domain, or product expert. Agree ahead of time what areas of questioning you and your colleague will pursue and, if you can, prepare some crucial questions. The best pre-sales consultants and support people I know have made questioning a fine art. They impress the prospect just by asking questions — insightful, probing, open-ended questions based on their knowledge of the industry, the prospect, and the prospect's competition.

MEETINGS AND PRESENTATIONS

Every meeting or presentation with a prospect warrants a plan, even if it's only five sentences long. It's really your sales plan in microcosm: (1) situation assessment, (2) objectives (yours and theirs), (3) strategy, and (4) tactics. You and your team members must understand all four components.

What are your roles during a meeting or presentation? That depends on you, your team, the audience, what your objectives are, where you are in your selling cycle, and the venue.

The first thing you must do is prepare, prepare, prepare. Here are some pointers:

▶ Before the meeting, contact the prospect to come up with a mutually acceptable agenda and objectives.

▶ For any presentation or demonstration, rehearse. Check your PC, screen-saver timeout, batteries or power cord, and room lights. Make sure you've got the right version of the

---

TACTIC: Plan for a rehearsal the afternoon before the presentation. At least two weeks in advance, give each team member a packet containing the sales plan and a checklist of things that could go wrong. By showing your concern with the details, you will motivate them not only to attend rehearsal but to be prepared for anything.

---

presentation. In case your PC crashes, have hard copies of your slides.

▶ Discuss with your team what objections might be raised and who will handle them. Do circumstances suggest they should be handled during the presentation? Or can you still be credible if you respond to the issues immediately after the presentation or even days later?

Here's how to handle the presentation itself:

▶ Address the points that are crucial to the prospect's business. Be brief, but not generic; you can't differentiate yourself by being generic.

▶ If your team members are strong enough, let them facilitate part of the meeting or presentation. Remember, though, you own that sales opportunity — not your team or your manager or your CEO. Your team's actions should communicate this to the prospect.

▶ Even if one person takes notes on a flip chart, have all your team members take notes during the event. Questions, concerns, ideas, action items, and especially audience comments should be captured for your debriefing immediately after the event.

TIER-LEVEL SELLING

Sometimes the seller's or buyer's company will require contacts to be made within a single level — your boss to your contact's boss, VP to VP, and so forth. This policy, known as tier-level selling, is common in Europe and Asia, where calling on your peer's boss is considered inappropriate. For expensive products and services in the United States, the same holds true; the prospect's CEO or CFO will usually want to establish a relationship with his counterpart in your company. This should not be something to avoid, but there are pitfalls you need to be aware of when executive management gets directly involved in your deal.

You need to communicate to the exec — as diplomatically as possible — that he is working for you on the sales opportunity, not the reverse. The best way to do this is to present a complete, well-thought-out strategic sales plan that specifies when, where, and how the exec will be involved.

When you've demonstrated that you've accurately assessed the sales opportunity and designed appropriate objectives, strategy, and tactics, the upper-level manager is more likely to follow your lead.

DEBRIEFING

Too few sales teams bother with this important step. It's usually, "Whew, that's over. Let's get to the airport and see if we can catch an early flight." Here is where your leadership is crucial. You need to let your team know in advance that there will be a debriefing, and you need to manage the session for best results. It's really not that difficult to answer several crucial questions (and take one further action):

1. Did we achieve our objectives, and the prospect's, for the meeting?

2. If not, where did we fall short, and why? What do we need to do about it? Who will follow up? When, how, and with whom?

3. If we did achieve the objectives, what could we have done better?

4. What new issues were raised? What do we need to do about them? Who will follow up? When, how, and with whom?

5. Review and validate the next step(s) in the sales plan.

As an individual sales rep, your skills and knowledge can bring you your share of business. But if you can organize and manage an effective virtual sales team to execute a team-oriented sales plan, keeping your eye on all the variables discussed here, you'll have gained another key component of sustainable competitive advantage.

Part

5

The Decision
and Beyond

The decision is at hand. You know what the outcome is going to be, since it was effectively your sales plan that was adopted by the evaluation team, although some of them didn't even know it. You've built business credibility with executives by stating in business terms how your offering will help achieve their business plan and by how much. The influence you've tapped has come through for you — handling objections when you weren't there, highlighting the strengths and downplaying the weaknesses of your offering, providing you with insights into how the decision makers were leaning, warning you of your competitors' moves. You've differentiated your offering and yourself and established your integrity and your value as a resource.

"Are you sure I'll be able to reach you after I sign this?"

Maybe you don't quite have the deal wired, but you know you're going to be selected. Your insiders tell you you're going to get beaten up on payment terms, the company will want you to assign certain key people to the project, and they'll squeeze another percent or two off your price — but the deal's yours. The decision has been made.

What happens now?

By the end of this final part of *How Winners Sell*

▶ you will understand how deals can be lost after they are won — and how to prevent it, and

▶ you'll know how to recruit, train, and utilize an apostle — an unassailable reference.

"And the Contract Goes To . . ."

▶ STRATEGY #20. DON'T STOP SELLING AFTER THE DECISION IS MADE

Have you ever won a deal, then immediately lost it? It's happened to many of us. We've learned all about buyers' remorse, and we've learned not to try to close the deal before we've addressed all the last-minute doubts and objections. But those aren't the only reasons we can lose a "done deal." Sometimes the competition

213
△

crawls in and undoes our deal, hoping that by stopping the process they can reverse the decision.

What do you do after the decision is announced but before the contract is signed? First, make sure you know exactly what has to be done to get your contract signed. This includes getting approval from legal, purchasing, the board, and the CEO. There are probably steps in the final approval process that weren't disclosed during evaluation because the people responsible for approval at that level didn't want salespeople to call on them. Who on the prospect's side, as well as yours, is responsible for each step? When must those steps be taken to ensure that the contract gets signed when the prospect promised?

Next, get in there and sell. Reassure them that they made the right decision. When the time is right, walk around with your sponsors and shake people's hands. Ask them to restate why they are buying from you. What made them feel secure? What concerns did they have about your competition? Assure them that you will be there for support as long as they need you (or until the handoff to post-sales, if that's how your company handles accounts).

Make sure that any appropriate post-decision meetings are scheduled right away and that they are on people's calendars. If your product or service delivery department isn't pushing hard enough, you'll need to take a bit more control. Make sure the decision is immersed in quick-drying cement.

Why do all this? Some of your competitors carry the "losing is not an option" philosophy pretty far. They'll figure that since they've already lost, they've got nothing to lose by trying to stop the prospect from signing with you — and they'll stop at nothing. The merely desperate will tell everybody they can get to, especially at the top levels, that

Each of these steps gets added to your tactical plan. See ch. 16.

Holden International calls this "advertising the order."

> "You may have to fight a battle more than once to win it."
>
> — MARGARET THATCHER

there's been a terrible mistake: "We must have put the decimal point in the wrong place. Let me refigure the price. I'm sure we can beat that guy's deal." The viciously dangerous will find a disgruntled former employee of your company — one who's eager to reveal where the bodies are hidden. Unheard of? It happens all the time. Be prepared.

It would be hard for an executive to switch to your competitor once she has personally walked you around headquarters to shake everybody's hand. That's exactly why you should do it. It's also a good time to connect with people who were against you, who supported your competitor. Spend some time with them; find out what you have to do to mend fences; address their doubts; reassure them that their opposition will not affect their relationship with you and your company. It's also important to give them a way to save face in the eyes of their colleagues — for example, by asking for their views on an issue or two.

Bury the hatchet with those who supported your competitor.

The thing to remember is to keep moving forward. Don't go on vacation just because the decision has been made. You can't take anything for granted.

My first job in technology, back around 1980, was with a gentleman who was, shall we say, rough around the edges. He was a brilliant programmer, a capable consultant, and a very persuasive salesman, but behind it all he was an astute businessman. Once he sold an accounts payable system to a company in White Plains, New York, and went to deliver the system himself. He installed the software, which he had developed over time for several other companies. Within a few hours, he had customized the code for the new client. After running a quick test to make sure it was working properly, he entered his own name and the amount of the client's final contract payment. Then he loaded checks into the printer, which he had instructed the client to order and deliver before he installed the software. Within seconds, out came check number one — for the balance due.

He walked over to the financial controller and showed him the check. "The program works," he said. "Would you sign this, so I can be on my way?"

The controller grimaced, then smiled, and then signed the check. It was arrogant behavior, granted, but this consultant instinctively knew to never stop selling. He wrote many more programs for that company over the years, and his work was a foundation upon which that company grew.

KNOW THY COMPETITOR, REVISITED

A question for you: What will your competitor do when he finds out your company has been selected? If you can't answer with any confidence, or if you haven't already taken steps to keep him from stealing your win, you are at risk.

Here are some time-tested ways the competition might "flip" your sale. Protect yourself against these tactics:

▶ **A dramatic price cut.** A competitor of one of my clients offered to give his product away free, hoping to make money later through service, upgrades, and add-ons.

▶ **Going over your contact's head.** Your competitor's CEO calls your prospect's CEO for a meeting and a chance to do some last-minute power bonding. If your competitor's CEO is well known, charismatic, or desperate, this sometimes works. I know of many cases where the competitor's VP of sales showed up at the prospect's headquarters, demanded a meeting, and wound up with the deal in hand.

▶ **The hatchet job.** Your competitor digs up some unflattering information about you — a customer defection, an

---

TACTIC: Speak with a key buyer in an account where you have won business. Ask him specifically what, if anything, your competition did to try to upset your victory. Chances are the competitor will try that again in another opportunity.

---

internal memo on product failure rates, a former employee's accusations — and hands it to a top influencer or decision maker. Your best approach is to be open and honest about it with the prospect. Above all, if there's bad news coming, you'd better be the first to tell it. Immunize them.

The message here is clear: Information is power. If you know what your competitor has done in the past, build yourself an ironclad, Teflon-coated, Kevlar-lined shield against those tactics. And do it well in advance, while you're selling, *not* after you've been proclaimed the winner.

Chapter 21

"Let Me Put You in Touch With ..."

► STRATEGY #21. TRANSFORM KEY CUSTOMERS INTO UNASSAILABLE REFERENCES

This book is about winning deals — plural, not singular. That's the natural order of things, anyway, because once you've closed a deal like the winners I've been writing about, you've laid the groundwork for the next deal, and the one after that. You've created the best, most powerful sales tool of all — a good reference.

"Good references are made, not born," says Olin Thompson, my trusted friend and colleague. He's right, of course. And that's what this chapter is about — turning customers into good references. In fact, into apostles.

References fall into two broad categories, which sometimes overlap: those your company maintains, and your personal references. Winners know how to use both to best effect. But, you may ask, if the company maintains references, why do you need your own? Several reasons:

▶ If your company doesn't manage its references well, you may not have a reliable advocate when you need one.

▶ The references your company maintains may not be in the region or industry you're selling to.

▶ Your company's references may not be in the right function or level to help you in the prospect's company.

▶ A company reference may not be willing to say what needs to be said.

You need personal references, because when company references won't do, you have to take the responsibility yourself. This means you have to develop and nurture your own, and you have to protect them. If winners are ever possessive, it is when asked to share their personal references with other salespeople. They believe that their personally developed references can be abused, and they're right. Goodwill can be used up.

> "An ardent supporter of the hometown team should go to a game prepared to take offense, no matter what happens."
>
> — ROBERT BENCHLEY

CARE AND FEEDING

Think of the practice of turning customers into unassailable references as a twelve-step program.

1. Earn your client's business and respect by winning the evaluation ethically and creatively. Be straight about what your product or service will do for his company, and be sure both parties see the result as a win-win relationship.

2. Target an appropriate candidate in the account to develop as a reference — ideally, but not necessarily, the high-level buyer who wrote the check for your product or service. Now take everything I just said in point one and see if it applies also to your potential reference. For example, if he feels you misrepresented something during the evaluation, he will not be convincing when he extols your virtues to your next prospect. By the way, enthusiasm and credibility are extremely valuable attributes for a reference.

3. Stay visible. Does your company require you to hand off new customers to a post-sales team? If so, you need to detour a bit from that structure. Set aside some time to stay connected with your candidate reference; call him regularly, sit in on occasional meetings, stop by just to say hello. Get copies of status reports from the post-sales delivery or service team and call the reference if something unexpected happens, whether positive or negative.

In an interview conducted in a 2001 study by WR Friend & Associates, a vice president of a $500 million food processing company said, "There is nothing worse than having the day you sign the contract be the last day you see the sales rep." I can assure you that most executives feel the same way.

4. Work in cooperation with your post-sales team, not against them. If there's an account executive responsible for your customer after the sale, make sure you build a win-win relationship with her as well.

5.   Keep track of the value your product or service is providing, in financial terms. This is nearly impossible for a sales rep to do alone; if you're lucky enough to work for a company that does it, get the numbers and discuss them with your reference. This will reassure him that going with your company was the right decision, and it will provide him with convincing data to give to your next prospect.

6.   Understand your reference's personal win. If he recommends you to a new prospect, what's in it for him? One of the most valuable things you can provide your reference, whatever his level in the organization, is education. Be his trusted advisor; filter, interpret, translate, and decipher information about his industry, competitors, customers, and suppliers. In exchange for his help, coach him on selling his ideas to his superiors. If you do this right, he'll be more valuable to his own organization.

7.   Train your reference. Whether he's the ally you recruited and trained to sell on your behalf, or someone you met after the contract was signed, you have to train him if you want him to be a good reference. He should know and be able to talk knowledgeably about

- ▶ your company's messages

- ▶ how and why your company was selected

- ▶ your competitors' strengths and weaknesses

- ▶ issues his company had with you and how those were favorably resolved

- ▶ instances where your company, and you in particular, went the extra mile to meet his company's requirements

- ▶ the standard sales objections your company faces, and responses to those objections

8.   Keep your reference informed. Don't ever let him be surprised by information about you during a reference call.

Brief your contact just as you would any other member of your team. Tell him

- ▶ with whom he will be speaking

- ▶ what that person's company does

- ▶ where the company is in its evaluation process

- ▶ what the prospect likes and dislikes about your offering

- ▶ who your competitors are, and how you want him to position you against those competitors

- ▶ which subjects he should defer to you

- ▶ which subjects he should raise with the prospect

9. Keep up your relationships with others in your reference account as well. If you've invested a lot of time in developing your reference and have learned to use him well, what would you do if he disappeared tomorrow? Is there someone who could step into his place?

10. Make sure your company takes care of your references. Without usurping the authority or responsibility of the post-sales team, make sure your reference receives special treatment — fast access to customer care, free tickets to your

---

TACTIC: Right now, identify contacts in two accounts and a specific tactical plan, including dates and actions, that will transform them into effective, unassailable references. Then execute the plan.

---

company's annual customer conference, or perhaps a regular round of golf with you and your company's CEO.

11. Use the reference regularly. Don't let months go by without making him feel useful. References grow stale through lack of use.

△

12. Make sure your reference is believable. My friend Olin reminds sales reps that if their reference's story sounds too perfect, his credibility goes out the window. It's good, not bad, for a reference to say, "There are two small issues that remain with XYZCo. They've done everything they promised, but these two things came up which they've been working to resolve. . . ."

One final note: While winning you new business, your reference may begin to wonder whether his own success will hurt him. Will he lose resources? Will he receive less attention from you or your company? Will someone else usurp his favored-reference spot? Bring the subject into the open from time to time. Reassure him that his success as a reference will only make him more valuable in your eyes.

The Book in Review

Now I've given you all twenty-one strategies that you'll need in your quest to outsell your competition and win big sales. Whether you've enjoyed sales superiority in the past or not, the real question is this: What are you going to do today, and tomorrow, and the next day?

If you've made it this far in the book, you've now arrived at a crossroads. It's time to act. You have a range of

225
△

options, from the incremental approach — incorporating a few of these tactics as part of your current sales efforts — to the equivalent of hitting Control-Alt-Delete and rebooting as someone else.

With that in mind, here's a summary list of behaviors and attributes that are the building blocks and mortar of winning — this time, from the point of view of your customer or client.

▶ Winners answer their customers' questions directly and truthfully. They prove their integrity by acting in their customers' best interests, never selling them anything that will not help the buyer's business. Knowing this, customers don't question winners' motives.

▶ Winners are accountable. Mistakes may be made and deadlines missed, but winners take responsibility and tell why it happened, what they are going to do about it, and why it will not happen again.

▶ Winners are diligent and expeditious. They want to earn, not just tie up, their clients' business, and they understand that time is money. They are on time for meetings, early with proposals, and prompt in responding to questions. Winners underpromise and overdeliver.

▶ Winners are methodical. They work from a plan, a behavior that comforts clients. Winners always know where they are going and how they will get there.

▶ Winners are responsive. Prospects understand that vendors who are not consistently available while selling will be unreachable with a signed contract in hand.

▶ Winners understand their clients' business goals and objectives. Having taken the time to listen, study, and explore, they can provide a clear vision in meaningful terms of how their offering, their company, and they themselves can help achieve the client's business plan.

▶ Winners ask powerful questions. They can reveal unforeseen ways of improving businesses and, on the principle that what you don't know *can* hurt you, probe for hidden risks.

▶ Winners mobilize resources. Whether it's their own CEO or a third party, they bring in the right person at the right time to help the customer.

▶ Winners add value — their expertise in the client's industry. They maintain an active network of industry associates, customers, and resources, attend meetings and conferences, know the issues, and can quote as well as debate the pundits and luminaries.

▶ Winners understand their clients' politics. They find influential people and give them reasons to help their selling efforts.

▶ Winners provide value on every call. Their name and their company's name are associated with value. Their phone calls get returned, and they get the meetings they request.

▶ Winners are technologically savvy, using the latest tools to deliver more value to their customers and to win more business.

▶ Winners are competitive, not only head-to-head with their sales rivals but in the customer's competitive interests as well.

That's clear enough, isn't it? If you hold these principles, strategies, and tactics in mind, you'll be well on your way to the winner's circle.

A final word of warning: There's powerful stuff here. Use it with care — and be magnanimous to the losers.

△

How to Get Your Project Funded

The contribution that follows is from a friend and colleague, Tim Noonan. Tim is president of The XSEL Group, Inc, a consultancy specializing in providing business and financial training and tools to selling organizations worldwide.

Capital investment is any outlay of money from which your customer expects future benefits. Capital investments differ from routine annual expenses in that the benefits derived from these investments continue into the future for approximately three to five years, or even longer. When your

229
△

customer invests in a new piece of production equipment or a new plant, the annual benefits could continue for many years. On the other hand, an existing customer may decide to make a capital investment in upgrading its computer systems, thus deriving benefits for five years or less, at which time they will need to be upgraded again to more advanced computers. The time span for derived benefits is based on the estimated useful life of the asset. Fast-changing technologies like computer systems usually have a useful life or write-off period of five years or less.

As a sales professional, it's important for you to know that capital investments are made by your customers to meet the following business goals:

▶ To satisfy their customers by providing specific products or services.

▶ To satisfy their owners (stockholders) by maximizing profits.

▶ To satisfy the public by being safe and environmentally correct.

You can help your customer meet these goals and objectives with your applications and solutions. What you need to understand and how you go about helping your customer determine the economic benefits of your proposed solution, especially if it requires a capital investment, is the most important activity you can engage in as a sales professional.

Capital investments are usually made for the following purposes:

▶ To improve productivity.

▶ To increase efficiency.

▶ To reduce overall costs.

▶ To enhance revenues.

▶ To increase quality.

▶ To strengthen competitive position.

As a sales professional, it's incumbent on you to assess the profit creation potential of your proposed solution in each of these areas. For example, if you claim you can improve the productivity of your customer's manufacturing process, you must be able to quantify or measure and relate the improvement in the value of usable or marketable output or the cost-effectiveness of a workforce in generating it. Either the value must go up or the cost must go down to certify a productivity gain. Reducing the contribution of labor content or reducing the level of skilled labor required, thereby reducing its expense, is one way. Increasing output per worker is the other. If you claim that you can strengthen your customer's competitive position through utilizing advanced technology in the order-entry fulfillment system that will improve customer satisfaction, then you must be able to show and demonstrate that this solution will allow your customer to better serve his customers. This could be demonstrated by speeding the process of getting customer orders into the system and consequently reducing overall cycle time. It is not enough to stop here. You must go to the next step and show or estimate the potential economic benefits, such as reduced inventory levels, reduced receivables, and potential for new business (due to reduced cycle time), to name just a few, which means increased revenue.

The area to be explored next is the process your customers use to decide on the best use of project funding or capital investments. In most companies, there are more proposals for projects than the firm is able or willing to finance. Each year your customers go through a capital budgeting process and set aside a certain amount of investment money. At any point in time there could be a few dozen or more proposals vying for this finite amount of investment funds. The total of the proposals will always far exceed the total amount budgeted. Some of these proposals will be good and others poor, and methods or processes must be developed for distinguishing between them. Essentially, the end result is a ranking of the proposals by IRR and business fit, and a cutoff point for determining how far down the ranked list to go. There are several processes your customers can use to make a final determination on which projects to fund. The essential steps are the following:

- ▶ Identify opportunities.

- ▶ Estimate the cost-benefit or total value.

- ▶ Evaluate the cost-benefit or total value.

- ▶ Weigh each opportunity.

- ▶ Decide on the best opportunities.

- ▶ Implement the best opportunities.

- ▶ Evaluate each investment.

As a sales professional, it is important for you to determine early in the sales cycle the critical nature of each project you engage in and where and how it fits with your customer's business goals. Then, craft your sales strategy to ensure closure of the business for you and value creation for your customer.

A powerful tool that you can use to show and demonstrate to the decision makers the financial value of your proposed project solution is a tool called Cost-Benefit ROI Analysis. If you use this tool correctly, it can have a major impact on the acceptance and success of your project. It will build your credibility and confidence level with customer managers and decision makers who understand and use this tool in evaluating the potential financial benefits of all capital projects. If used properly, it can also substantially reduce your selling cycle and increase your sales margins.

There is nothing difficult or mysterious about cost-benefit or return-on-investment analysis. The math involved is not difficult. You perform a cost-benefit analysis every time you decide to move $100 out of your bank account earning only 2.5 percent per year into a certificate of deposit (CD) that earns 4 percent per year. You make that decision because you know that every $100 you move into the CD will earn $1.50 per year more than it would have otherwise.

Cost-benefit ROI analysis is a measure that tells your customer what it will cost him to receive a benefit from the proposed capital investment. The formula is quite simple:

$$\frac{\text{Project Cost}}{\text{Project Benefit}} = \text{ROI}$$

Cost-Benefit ROI Analysis								
	Initial	Year 1	Year 2	Year 3	Year 4	Year 5	Total	
Investment/Cost:								
• Mobile Telephone								
• Equipment	($30)						($30)	1
•								
•								
•								
Total Investment/Cost	($30)						($30)	
Operating Expenses:								
• Cellular Air Time		($48)	($48)	($48)	($48)	($48)	($240)	2
• Depreciation Expense		($6)	($6)	($6)	($6)	($6)	($30)	
•								
•								
Total Operating Expenses		($54)	($54)	($54)	($54)	($54)	($270)	
Benefits:								
• Incremental Revenue		$160	$160	$160	$160	$160	$800	3
•								
•								
•								
•								
Total Benefits		$160	$160	$160	$160	$160	$800	
Profit Creation:								4
Profit Before Tax (PBT)		$106	$106	$106	$106	$106	$530	
Less Taxes (@ 35%)		($37)	($37)	($37)	($37)	($37)	($185)	
Profit After Tax (PAT)		$69	$69	$69	$69	$69	$345	
Add Back Deprec. &		$6	$6	$6	$6	$6	$0	
Cash Flow	($30)	$75	$75	$75	$75	$75	$345	5
Cumulative Cash Flow	($30)	$45	$120	$195	$270	$345		
NPV @ 10%	($30)	$68	$62	$56	$51	$47	$254	6
IRR	250%							7
Payback (Months)	5 Mo.'s.							8

(1) shows the $30,000 initial investment in a mobile telephone system.

△

(2) shows the ongoing incremental expense of cellular airtime ($48,000) of the initial investment. Depreciation was calculated using the straight-line method of 20 percent per year.
($30,000 x 20% = $6,000 per year for five years)

(3) shows the yearly incremental benefits of a mobile telephone system, which is incrementally $160,000 per year.

(4) shows the profit before tax (PBT) of $160,000.
(total benefits minus total expenses)

shows the annual tax implication of 35 percent on the PBT.
($106,000 x 35% = $37,000)

shows the annual profit after tax (PAT).
($106,000 minus $37,000 = $69,000)

(5) shows the initial and ongoing cash flows (both outflows and inflows) from the investment.

(6) shows the NPV using a cost of capital or discount factor of 10 percent. The discount factor is applied to each year's cash flow figures. For an investment to be attractive, the NPV must be zero or greater. In this illustration, the NPV is a positive $254,000 and is truly an outstanding investment.

(7) shows that the IRR or ROI on this investment is 250 percent.

(8) shows the payback of the investment of five months. Payback is the number of months or years required to return the original investment.

For your proposed investments (solutions) to succeed, you first must determine what key business results your customer wants to achieve: higher customer retention, shorter sales cycles, or lower investment in inventory, for example. Next, identify and map all the processes that go into making that happen. For example, let's assume that you have a solution that will result in a higher customer retention rate.

A higher customer retention rate depends on higher customer satisfaction. Satisfaction is derived from successful interaction with the customers. What processes in your customer's organization pertain to customer interaction? Ringing up sales at the checkout counter? Processing catalog orders? Answering the customer support phone lines? Once you understand how your customer operates, you will be able to pinpoint the processes that drive his success; you will then be in a good position to recommend improvements to those processes.

Mapping processes — benchmarking the cost of processes — as they are currently handled, will help you distill which of your solutions will have a real impact on your customer's bottom line.

For you to create customer value, your solution must add measurable improvements to the process. If you first measure the cost of your customer's current processes, it's easy to quantify the value of the improvements you hope to achieve.

The following quote from Lord Kelvin, one of the world's most renowned mathematicians, sums up the importance of quantifying the value you create for your customers: "When you can measure what you are speaking about and express it in numbers, you know something about it; but when you cannot express it in numbers, your knowledge is of a meager and unsatisfactory kind."

Appendix 2

Resources

RESEARCH ASSISTANCE

www.spireproject.com
www.refdesk.com

BUSINESS INFORMATION PORTALS

www.ceoexpress.com
www.brint.com
www.executivelibrary.com

DAILY BUSINESS NEWS

www.HowWinnersSell.com
(links to web-based news services)

TELEPHONE AND ADDRESSES

www.555-1212.com
www.switchboard.com

INFORMATION ABOUT COMPANIES

www.hoovers.com (subscription)
www.freeedgar.com
www.sec.gov
finance.yahoo.com
www.lexis-nexis.com (subscription)

INFORMATION ABOUT INDUSTRIES

www.verticalnet.com
www.brint.com

SEARCH ENGINES

www.alltheweb.com
www.av.com
www.google.com

BUSINESS MAGAZINES

Fortune	www.fortune.com
Forbes	www.forbes.com
Business 2.0	www.business20.com
The Wall Street Journal	www.wsj.com
Fast Company	www.fastcompany.com
Red Herring	www.redherring.com
BusinessWeek	www.businessweek.com

BOOKS

www.TheSteinAdvantage.com (click Bibliography)

Index

Notes

Notes

Notes

Notes

► Acknowledgments

Thanks to my editor, Jeff Morris, who brilliantly and tirelessly transformed what I wrote into what I really wanted to say.

Thanks to my publisher, Ray Bard, a truly wise man.

Thanks to the brain trust who unselfishly gave their time to read some or all of the first draft and who provided me with honest, invaluable feedback: Bruce Bond, Mike Clayville, Tony Friscia, Gerhard Gschwandtner, Brad Helmer, Andy Mank, Audrey Melkin, Kathleen Seacat, Vicki Scott, Lee Marc Stein, Steve Waterhouse, Alan Weiss, Robert Workman, and John Zobel.

Thanks to these dear people, without whose encouragement the book might have ground to a halt anywhere along the way, if it ever got started at all: Joy Baldridge, Larry Berk, Eileen Campanelli, Barry Davis, Diane Engel, Ralph Engel, Peter Gamar, Marty Katz, LaVon Koerner, Snowden McFall, Tim Noonan ("Dave, you need to write a book"), Alex Polner, and Petra Williams.

Thanks to my friends and colleagues who contributed directly to *How Winners Sell*: Bob DeGroot, Bill Friend, Aaron Johnson, Dan Kossmann, Lisa Napolitano, Tim Noonan, Ari Pollack, Olin Thompson, Gary Toole, and Steve Waterhouse.

Thanks to more friends and colleagues who contributed in many other ways to *How Winners Sell*: Al Barrenechea, Chris Caparon, Doug Carabillo, Tom Connellan, Kerry Evans, Bob Frare, Paul Goldner, Helen Grogan, Nick Haley, Rick Hartung, Gerry O'Connell, Jim Schappert, David Scott, Lori Slater, and all the winners with whom I have had the pleasure of working.

Thanks to all those whose influence on me led to not only my writing of *How Winners Sell* but the parts of me that it contains: Steve Andersen, John Andrus, Ken Arnold, Rick Benoit, Johanna Bohoy, Dan Brown, Mike Campanelli, Gary Davies, Dave Evans, Chris Fountain, Alan Ganapol, Frank Grywalski, Mack Hanan, Dave Hathaway, Jim Holden, Gabrielle Bernhard Jackson, John Koontz, Andy Lavelle, Paul Margolis, Duncan McLeod, Jeff Miller, Rick Morris, Rick Page, Eric Pesak, Mark Schermers, Andy Schor, Steve Shorten, Lee Marc Stein, Nancy Stephens, Dick Whitney, Mark Williams, and Art Zuckerman.

And of course, most important, thanks to my wife, business partner, and best friend, Vivian, for all the encouragement, support, insight, persistence, grunt work, and sanity checks.

About the Author

Before he founded his consultancy, The Stein Advantage, Inc., in 1997, Dave Stein was employed by several leading-edge high-tech companies in a diversity of roles: programmer, systems engineer, sales representative, sales manager, director of worldwide sales development, VP of sales, VP of marketing, VP of international operations, VP of client services, and VP of strategic alliances.

During the early 1990s, Dave lived and sold in Europe, commencing international operations for the technology company he helped to build, Datalogix International, which was later acquired by Oracle. In the decade since, Dave has focused on coaching experienced sales teams in 48 states and 20 countries. His unique skills in competitive sales strategies and political positioning have helped thousands of sales professionals win hundreds of millions of dollars of business against insurmountable odds. Specializing in large, complex opportunities, Dave is much in demand as a speaker, consultant, coach, and trainer. He has worked with companies small and large, from $5 million in sales to the Fortune 100, including IBM, Oracle, Hewlett-Packard, Invensys plc, NEC, ALLTEL, Pitney Bowes, and Bayer. He sits on the board of directors of Global Entertainment Holdings/Equities, Inc., a publicly held company.

Dave is a fitness enthusiast, instrument-rated pilot, airplane owner, bicyclist, skydiver, scuba diver, firewalker, early adopter of technology, and recognized expert on business-to-business sales, marketing, and service. He is a member of the National Speakers Association and the Strategic Account Management Association. Dave is a native New Yorker with two grown daughters. He and his wife, Vivian, live and work north of New York City and on Martha's Vineyard, Massachusetts, with two cats and a golden retriever.

▶ The Stein Advantage

Founded in 1997 as a sales consultancy, The Stein Advantage, Inc., coaches companies to win large accounts in highly competitive sales environments. The New York–based consultancy works with CEOs, vice presidents of sales, business development, marketing executives, sales managers, sales support staffs, and sales professionals alike, helping clients large and small in a wide range of sales-related business projects.

The Stein Advantage is about business value. For some clients, that value comes from dramatically improving sales effectiveness by way of a practical, strategic sales process; for others, by developing a sales-oriented culture that improves competitiveness and boosts top-line revenues.

Larger companies leverage The Stein Advantage's diagnostic and remedial expertise to overcome tough competitors, motivate their sales forces, and refocus their selling efforts to achieve new levels of credibility and differentiation with higher-level executives to whom they are selling.

In addition to devising winning sales strategies, Stein Advantage clients produce more exciting and effective demos, hard-hitting executive presentations, impressive corporate visits, and financially compelling proposals. They gain skill and insight into effective recruiting practices, and they discover that aligning sales, delivery, and marketing to a common vision can result in a team that wins.

The Stein Advantage continues to anticipate and adapt to a changing environment. It now offers *How Winners Sell* in audio, web, classroom, and personal learning media. Even as businesses all over the world wrestle with intensified economic, geopolitical, and competitive influences that constantly change the way business is done, The Stein Advantage believes that the old saying still holds true: Nothing happens until someone sells something.

To contact The Stein Advantage, call 845-621-4100, fax 845-621-3723, or e-mail info@TheSteinAdvantage.com.